The Poetry of Hannah More

Volume I

Hannah More was born on February 2nd, 1745 at Fishponds in the parish of Stapleton, near Bristol. She was the fourth of five daughters.

The City of Bristol, at that time, was a centre for slave-trading and Hannah would, over time, become one of its staunchest critics.

She was keen to learn, possessed a sharp intellect and was assiduous in studying. Hannah first wrote in 1762 with The Search after Happiness (by the mid-1780s some 10,000 copies had been sold).

In 1767 Hannah became engaged to William Turner. After six years, with no wedding in sight, the engagement was broken off. Turner then bestowed upon her an annual annuity of £200. This was enough to meet her needs and set her free to pursue a literary career.

Her first play, The Inflexible Captive, was staged at Bath in 1775. The famous David Garrick himself produced her next play, Percy, in 1777 as well as writing both the Prologue and Epilogue for it. It was a great success when performed at Covent Garden in December of that year.

Hannah turned to religious writing with Sacred Dramas in 1782; it rapidly ran through nineteen editions. These and the poems Bas-Bleu and Florio (1786) mark her gradual transition to a more serious and considered view of life.

Hannah contributed much to the newly-founded Abolition Society including, in February 1788, her publication of Slavery, a Poem recognised as one of the most important of the abolition period.

Her work now became more evangelical. In the 1790s she wrote several Cheap Repository Tracts which covered moral, religious and political topics and were both for sale or distributed to literate poor people. The most famous is, perhaps, The Shepherd of Salisbury Plain, describing a family of incredible frugality and contentment. Two million copies of these were circulated, in one year.

In 1789, she purchased a small house at Cowslip Green in Somerset. She was instrumental in setting up twelve schools in the area by 1800.

She continued to oppose slavery throughout her life, but at the time of the Abolition Bill of 1807, her health did not permit her to take as active a role in the movement as she had done in the late 1780s, although she maintained a correspondence with Wilberforce and others.

In July 1833, the Bill to abolish slavery throughout the British Empire passed in the House of Commons, followed by the House of Lords on August 1st.

Hannah More died on September 7th, 1833.

Index of Contents

The Slave Trade, A Poem

If heaven has into being deign'd to call
Thy light, O Liberty! to shine on all;
Bright intellectual Sun! why does thy ray
To earth distribute only partial day?
Since no resisting cause from spirit flows
Thy penetrating essence to opose;
No obstacles by Nature's hand imprest,

Thy subtle and ethereal beams arrest;
Nor motion's laws can speed thy active course,
Nor strong repulsion's pow'rs obstruct thy force;
Since there is no convexity in Mind,
Why are thy genial beams to parts confin'd?
While the chill North with thy bright ray is blest,
Why should fell darkness half the South invest?
Was it decreed, fair Freedom! at thy birth,
That thou shou'd'st ne'er irradiate all the earth?
While Britain basks in thy full blaze of light,
Why lies sad Afric quench'd in total night?
Thee only, sober Goddess! I attest,
In smiles chastis'd, and decent graces drest.
Not that unlicens'd monster of the crowd,
Whose roar terrific bursts in peals so loud,
Deaf'ning the ear of Peace: fierce Faction's tool;
Of rash Sedition born, and mad Misrule;
Whose stubborn mouth, rejecting Reason's rein,
No strength can govern, and no skill restrain;
Whose magic cries the frantic vulgar draw
To spurn at Order, and to outrage Law;
To tread on grave Authority and Pow'r,
And shake the work of ages in an hour:
Convuls'd her voice, and pestilent her breath,
She raves of mercy, while she deals out death:
Each blast is fate; she darts from either hand
Red conflagration o'er th' astonish'd land;
Clamouring for peace, she rends the air with noise,
And to reform a part, the whole destroys.
O, plaintive Southerne! whose impassion'd strain
So oft has wak'd my languid Muse in vain!
Now, when congenial themes her cares engage,
She burns to emulate thy glowing page;
Her failing efforts mock her fond desires,
She shares thy feelings, not partakes thy fires.
Strange pow'r of song! the strain that warms the heart
Seems the same inspiration to impart;
Touch'd by the kindling energy alone,
We think the flame which melts us is our own;
Deceiv'd, for genius we mistake delight,
Charm'd as we read, we fancy we can write.
Tho' not to me, sweet Bard, thy pow'rs belong
Fair Truth, a hallow'd guide! inspires my song.
Here Art wou'd weave her gayest flow'rs in vain,
For Truth the bright invention wou'd disdain.
For no fictitious ills these numbers flow,
But living anguish, and substantial woe;
No individual griefs my bosom melt,

For millions feel what Oronoko felt:
Fir'd by no single wrongs, the countless host
I mourn, by rapine dragg'd from Afric's coast.
Perish th'illiberal thought which wou'd debase
The native genius of the sable race!
Perish the proud philosophy, which sought
To rob them of the pow'rs of equal thought!
Does then th' immortal principle within
Change with the casual colour of a skin?
Does matter govern spirit? or is mind
Degraded by the form to which 'tis join'd?
No: they have heads to think, and hearts to feel,
And souls to act, with firm, tho' erring, zeal;
For they have keen affections, kind desires,
Love strong as death, and active patriot fires;
All the rude energy, the fervid flame,
Of high-soul'd passion, and ingenuous shame:
Strong, but luxuriant virtues boldly shoot
From the wild vigour of a savage root.
Nor weak their sense of honour's proud control,
For pride is virtue in a Pagan soul;
A sense of worth, a conscience of desert,
A high, unbroken haughtiness of heart:
That self-same stuff which erst proud empires sway'd,
Of which the conquerers of the world were made.
Capricious fate of man! that very pride
In Afric scourg'd, in Rome was deify'd.
No Muse, O Quashi! shall thy deeds relate,
No statue snatch thee from oblivious fate!
For thou wast born where never gentle Muse
On Valour's grave the flow'rs of Genius strews;
And thou wast born where no recording page
Plucks the fair deed from Time's devouring rage.
Had Fortune plac'd thee on some happier coast,
Where polish'd souls heroic virtue boast,
To thee, who sought'st a voluntary grave,
Th' uninjur'd honours of thy name to save,
Whose generous arm thy barbarous Master spar'd,
Altars had smok'd, and temples had been rear'd.
Whene'er to Afric's shores I turn my eyes,
Horrors of deepest, deadliest guilt arise;
I see, by more than Fancy's mirrow shewn,
The burning village, and the blazing town:
See the dire victim torn from social life,
The shrieking babe, the agonizing wife!
She, wretch forlorn! is dragg'd by hostile hands,
To distant tyrants sold, in distant lands!
Transmitted miseries, and successive chains,

The sole sad heritage her child obtains!
Ev'n this last wretched boon their foes deny,
To weep together, or together die.
By felon hands, by one relentless stroke,
See the fond links of feeling nature broke!
The fibres twisting round a parent's heart,
Torn from their grasp, and bleeding as they part.
Hold, murderers, hold! not aggravate distress;
Respect the passions you yourselves possess;
Ev'n you, of ruffian heart, and ruthless hand,
Love your own offspring, love your native land.
Ah! leave them holy Freedom's cheering smile,
The heav'n-taught fondness for the parent soil;
Revere affections mingled with our frame,
In every nature, every clime the same;
In all, these feelings equal sway maintain;
In all the love of Home and Freedom reign:
And Tempe's vale, and parch'd Angola's sand,
One equal fondness of their sons command.
Th' unconquer'd Savage laughs at pain and toil,
Basking in Freedom's beams which gild his native soil.
Does thirst of empire, does desire of fame,
(For these are specious crimes) our rage inflame?
No: sordid lust of gold their fate controls,
The basest appetite of basest souls;
Gold, better gain'd, by what their ripening sky,
Their fertile fields, their arts and mines supply.
What wrongs, what injuries does Opression plead
To smooth the horror of th' unnatural deed?
What strange offence, what aggravated sin?
They stand convicted-of a darker skin!
Barbarians, hold! th' opprobious commerce spare,
Respect his sacred image which they bear:
Tho' dark and savage, ignorant and blind,
They claim the common privilege of kind;
Let Malice strip them of each other plea,
They still are men, and men shou'd still be free.
Insulted Reason, loaths th' inverted trade -
Dire change! the agent is the purchase made!
Perplex'd, the baffled Muse involves the tale;
Nature confounded, well may language fail!
The outrag'd Goddess with abhorrent eyes
Sees Man the traffic, Souls the merchandize!
Plead not, in reason's palpable abuse,
Their sense of feeling callous and obtuse:
From heads to hearts lies Nature's plain appeal,
Tho' few can reason, all mankind can feel.
Tho' wit may boast a livelier dread of shame,

A loftier sense of wrong refinement claim;
Tho' polished manners may fresh wants invent,
And nice distinctions nicer souls torment;
Tho' these on finer spirits heavier fall,
Yet natural evils are the same to all.

Tho' wounds there are which reason's force may heal,
There needs no logic sure to make us feel.
The nerve, howe'er untutor'd, can sustain
A sharp, unutterable sense of pain;
As exquisitely fashion'd in a slave,
As where unequal fate a sceptre gave.
Sense is as keen where Congo's sons preside,
As where proud Tiber rolls his classic tide.
Rhetoric or verse may point the feeling line,
They do not whet sensation, but define.
Did ever slave less feel the galling chain,
When Zeno prov'd there was no ill in pain?
Their miseries philosophic quirks deride,
Slaves groan in pangs disown'd by Stoic pride.
When the fierce Sun darts vertical his beams,
And thirst and hunger mix their wild extremes;
When the sharp iron wounds his inmost soul,
And his strain'd eyes in burning anguish roll;
Will the parch'd negro find, ere he expire,
No pain in hunger, and no heat in fire?
For him, when fate his tortur'd frame destroys,
What hope of present fame, or future joys?
For this, have heroes shorten'd nature's date;
For that, have martyrs gladly met their fate;
But him, forlorn, no hero's pride sustains,
No martyr's blissful visions sooth his pains;
Sullen, he mingles with his kindred dust,
For he has learn'd to dread the Christian's trust;
To him what mercy can that Pow'r display,
Whose servants murder, and whose sons betray?
Savage! thy venial error I deplore,
They are not Christians who infest thy shore.
O thou sad spirit, whose preposterous yoke
The great deliver Death, at length, has broke!
Releas'd from misery, and escap'd from care,
Go meet that mercy man deny'd thee here.
In thy dark home, sure refuge of th' opress'd,
The wicked vex not, and the weary rest.
And, if some notions, vague and undefin'd,
Of future terrors have assail'd thy mind;
If such thy masters have presum'd to teach,
As terrors only they are prone to preach;

(For shou'd they paint eternal Mercy's reign,
Where were th' oppressor's rod, the captive's chain?)
If, then, thy troubled soul has learn'd to dread
The dark unknown thy trembling footsteps tread;
On Him, who made thee what thou art, depend;
He, who withholds the means, accepts the end.
Not thine the reckoning dire of Light abus'd,
Knowledge disgrac'd, and Liberty misus'd;
On thee no awful judge incens'd shall sit
For parts perverted, and dishonour'd wit.
Where ignorance will be found the surest plea,
How many learn'd and wise shall envy thee!

And thou, White Savage! whether lust of gold,
Or lust of conquest, rule thee uncontrol'd!
Hero, or robber!-by whatever name
Thou plead thy impious claim to wealth or fame;
Whether inferior mischiefs be thy boast,
A petty tyrant rifling Gambia's coast:
Or bolder carnage track thy crimson way,
Kings dispossess'd, and Provinces thy prey;
Panting to tame wide earth's remotest bound;
All Cortez murder'd, all Columbus found;
O'er plunder'd realms to reign, detested Lord,
Make millions wretched, and thyself abhorr'd; -
In Reason's eye, in Wisdom's fair account,
Your sum of glory boasts a like amount;
The means may differ, but the end's the same;
Conquest is pillage with a nobler name.
Who makes the sum of human blessings less,
Or sinks the stock of general happiness,
No solid fame shall grace, no true renown,
His life shall blazon, or his memory crown.
Had those advent'rous spirits who explore
Thro' ocean's trackless wastes, the far-sought shore;
Whether of wealth insatiate, or of pow'r,
Conquerors who waste, or ruffians who devour:
Had these possess'd, O Cook! thy gentle mind,
Thy love of arts, thy love of humankind;
Had these pursued thy mild and liberal plan,
Discovers had not been a curse to man!
The, bless'd Philanthropy! thy social hands
Had link'd dissever'd worlds in brothers bands;
Careless, if colour, or if clime divide;
Then, lov'd, and loving, man had liv'd, and died.
The purest wreaths which hang on glory's shrine,
For empires founded, peaceful Penn! are thine;
No blood-stain'd laurels crown'd thy virtuous toil,

No slaughter'd natives drench'd thy fair-earn'd soil.
Still thy meek spirit in thy flock survives,
Consistent still, their doctrines rule their lives;
Thy followers only have effac'd the shame
Inscrib'd by Slavery on the Christian name.
Shall Britain, where the soul of freedom reigns,
Forge chains for others she herself disdains?
Forbid it, Heaven! O let the nations know
The liberty she loves she will bestow;
Not to herself the glorious gift confin'd,
She spreads the blessing wide as humankind;
And, scorning narrow views of time and place,
Bids all be free in earth's extended space.
What page of human annals can record
A deed so bright as human rights restor'd?
O may that god-like deed, that shining page,
Redeem Our fame, and consecrate Our age!
And see, the cherub Mercy from above,
Descending softly, quits the sphere of love!
On feeling hearts she sheds celestial dew,
And breathes her spirit o'er th' enlighten'd few;
From soul to soul the spreading influence steals,
Till every breast the soft contagion feels.
She bears, exulting, to the burning shore
The loveliest office Angel ever bore;
To vindicate the pow'r in Heaven ador'd,
To still the clank of chains, and sheathe the sword;
To cheer the mourner, and with soothing hands
From bursting hearts unbind th' Oppressor's bands;
To raise the lustre of the Christian name,
And clear the foulest blot that dims its fame.
As the mild Spirit hovers o'er the coast,
A fresher hue the wither'd landscapes boast;
Her healing smiles the ruin'd scenes repair,
And blasted Nature wears a joyous air.
She spreads her blest commission from above,
Stamp'd with the sacred characters of love;
She tears the banner stain'd with blood and tears,
And, Liberty! thy shining standard rears!
As the bright ensign's glory she displays,
See pale Oppression faints beneath the blaze!
The giant dies! no more his frown appals,
The chain untouch'd, drops off; the fetter falls.
Astonish'd echo tells the vocal shore,
Opression's fall'n, and Slavery is no more!
The dusky myriads crowd the sultry plain,
And hail that mercy long invok'd in vain.

Victorious Pow'r! she bursts their tow-fold bands,
And Faith and Freedom spring from Mercy's hands.

On A Young Lady

Go, peaceful shade! exchange for sin and care
The glorious palm which patient suff'rers wear!
Go, take the meed victorious meekness gains,
Go, wear the crown triumphant faith obtains.
Those silent graces which the good conceal,
The day of dread disclosure shall reveal;
Then shall thy mild, retiring virtues rise,
And God, both judge and witness, give the prize.

War

O War, What art thou?
After the brightest conquest, what remains
Of all thy glories? For the vanquish'd - chains -
For the proud victor - what? Alas! to reign
O'er desolated nations - a drear waste,
By one man's crime, by one man's lust of power,
Unpeopled! Naked plains and ravaged fields,
Succeed to smiling harvests and the fruits
Of peaceful olive - luscious fig and vine!
Here, rifled temples are the cavern'd dens
Of savage beasts, or haunt of birds obscene;
There, populous cities blacken in the sun,
And in the general wreck proud palaces
Lie undistinguish'd, save by the dun smoke
Of recent conflagration! When the song
Of dear-bought joy, with many a triumph swell'd,
Salutes the victory's ear, and soothes his pride,
How is the grateful harmony profaned
With the sad dissonance of virgins' cries,
Who mourn their brothers slain! Of matrons hoar,
Who clasp their wither'd hands, and fondly ask
With iteration shrill - their slaughter'd sons!
How is the laurel's verdure stain'd with blood
And soil'd with widows' tears!

Inscription In A Beautiful Retreat Called Fairy Bower

Airy spirits, you who love
Cooling bower, or shady grove;
Streams that murmur as they flow,
Zephyrs bland that softly blow;

Babbling echo, or the tale
Of the love-lorn Nightingale;
Hither, airy spirits, come,
This is your peculiar home.

If you love a verdant glade,
If you love a noon-tide shade,
Hither, Sylphs and Fairies fly,
Unobserved of earthly eye.

Come, and wander every night,
By the moon-beam's glimmering light;
And again at early day
Brush the silver dews away.

Mark where first the daisies blow,
Where the bluest violets grow,
Where the sweetest linnet sings,
Where the earliest cowslip springs;

Where the largest acorn lies,
Precious in a Fairy's eyes:
Sylphs, thought unconfined to place,
Love to fill an acorn's space.

Come, and mark within what bush
Builds the blackbird or the thrush;
Great his joy who first espies,
Greater his who spares the prize!

Come, and watch the hallow'd bower,
Chase the insect from the flower;
Little offices like these,
Gentle souls and Fairies please.

Mortals! form'd of grosser clay,
From our haunts keep far away;
Or, if you should dare appear,
See that you from vice are clear.

Folly's minion, Fashion's fool,
Mad Ambition's restless tool!

Slave of passion, slave of power,
Fly, ah fly! this tranquil bower!

Son of avarice, soul of frost,
Wretch! of Heaven abhorr'd the most,
Learn to pity others' wants,
Or avoid these hallow'd haunts.

Eye unconscious of a tear,
When affliction's train appear:
Heart that never heaved a sigh
For another, come not nigh.

But, ye darling sons of Heaven,
Giving freely what was given;
You, whose liberal hands dispense
The blessings of benevolence:

You, who wipe the tearful eye,
You, who stop the rising sigh;
You, whose souls have understood
The luxury of doing good.

Come, ye happy virtuous few,
Open is my bower to you;
You, these mossy banks may press;
You, each guardian Fay shall bless.

Here and There

Here bliss is short, imperfect, insincere,
But total, absolute, and perfect there.
Here time's a moment, short our happiest state,
There infinite duration is our date.
Here Satan tempts, and troubles e'en the best,
In a weak sinful body here I dwell,
But there I drop this frail and sickly shell.
Here my best thoughts are stain'd with guilt and fear,
But love and pardon shall be perfect there.
Here my best duties are defiled with sin,
There all is ease without and peace within.
Here feeble faith supplies my only light,
There faith and hope are swallow'd up in sight.
Here love of self my fairest work destroys,
There love of God shall perfect all my joys.
Here things, as in a glass, are darkly shown,

There I shall know as clearly as I'm known.
Frail are the fairest flowers which bloom below,
There freshest palms on roots immortal grow.
Here wants or cares perplex my anxious mind,
But spirits there a calm fruition find.
Here disappointments my best schemes destroy,
There those that sow'd in tears shall reap in joy.
Here vanity is stamp'd on all below,
Perfection there one very good shall grow.
Here my fond heart is fasten'd on some friend,
Whose kindness may, whose life must have an end.
But there no failure can I ever prove,
God cannot disappoint, for God is love.
Here Christ for sinners suffer'd, groan'd, and bled,
But there he reigns the great triumphant head:
Here mock'd and scourged, he wore a crown of thorns,
A crown of glory there his brow adorns.
Here error clouds the will, and dims the sight,
There all is knowledge, purity and light.
Here so imperfect is this mortal state,
If blest myself I mourn some other's fate.
At every human wo I here repine,
The joy of every saint shall there be mine.
Here if I lean, the world shall pierce my heart,
But there that broken reed and I shall part.
Here on no promised good can I depend,
But there the Rock of Ages is my friend.
Here if some sudden joy delight inspire,
The dread to lose it damps the rising fire;
But there whatever good the soul employ,
The thought that 'tis eternal, crowns the joy.

Ode to Charity

O Charity, divinely wise,
Thou meek-ey'd Daughter of the skies
From the pure fountain of eternal light,
Where fair, immutable, and ever bright,
The beatific vision shines,
Where Angel with Archangel joins
In choral songs to sing his praise,
Parent of Life, Ancient of Days,
Who was ere Time existed, shall be
Thro' the wide round of vast Eternity,
O come, thy warm celestial beams impart,
Enlarge my feelings, and expand my heart!

Descend from radiant realms above,
Thou effluence of that boundless love
Whence joy and peace in streams unsully'd flow,
O deign to make thy lov'd abode below!
Tho' sweeter strains adorn'd my tongue
Than Saint conceiv'd or Seraph sung,
And tho' my glowing Fancy caught
Whatever Art or Nature taught,
Yet if this hard unfeeling heart of mine
Ne'er felt thy force, O Charity divine!
An empty shadow Science would be found:
My knowledge ignorance, my wit a sound!

Tho' my prophetic spirit knew
To bring futurity to view,
Without thy aid e'en this would nought avail,
For Tongues shall cease, and Prophecies shall fail.
Come then, thou sweet immortal guest,
Shed thy soft influence o'er my breast,
Bring with thee Faith, divinely bright,
And Hope, fair harbinger of light,
To clear each mist with their pervading ray,
To fit my soul for Heaven, and point the way;
There Perfect Happiness her sway maintains;
For there the God of peace for ever reigns.

The Bas Bleu: Or, Conversation. Addressed To Mrs. Vesey

VESEY, of Verse the judge and friend,
Awhile my idle strain attend:
Not with the days of early Greece,
I mean to ope my slender piece;
The rare Symposium to proclaim
Which crown'd th' Athenians' social name;
Or how Aspasia's parties shone,
The first Bas-bleu at Athens known;
Where SOCRATES unbending sat,
With ALCIBIADES in chat;
And PERICLES vouchsafed to mix
Taste, wit, and mirth, with politics.
Nor need I stop my tale to show,
At least to readers such as you,
How all that Rome esteem'd polite,
Supp'd with LUCULLUS every night;
LUCULLUS, who, from Pontus come,

Brought conquests, and brought cherries home.
Name but the suppers in th' Appollo,
What classic images will follow!
How wit flew round, while each might take
Conchylia from the Lucrine lake;
And Attic Salt, and Garum Sauce,
And Lettuce from the Isle of Cos;
The first and last from Greece transplanted,
Us'd here--because the rhyme I wanted:
How pheasant's heads, with cost collected,
And Phenicopters' stood neglected,
To laugh at SCIPIO's lucky hit,
POMPEY's bon-mot, or CAESAR's wit!
Intemperance, list'ning to the tale,
Forgot the Mullet growing stale;
And Admiration, balanc'd, hung
'Twixt PEACOCKS' brains, and TULLY's tongue.
I shall not stop to dwell on these,
But be as epic as I please,
And plunge at once in medias res.
To prove that privilege I plead,
I'll quote some Greek I cannot read;
Stunn'd by Authority you yield,
And I, not reason, keep the field.
Long was Society o'er-run
By Whist, that desolating Hun;
Long did Quadrille despotic sit,
That Vandal of colloquial wit;
And Conversation's setting light
Lay half-obscur'd in Gothic night.
At length the mental shades decline,
Colloquial wit begins to shine;
Genius prevails, and Conversation
Emerges into Reformation.
The vanquish'd triple crown to you,
BOSCAWEN sage, bright MONTAGU,
Divided, fell;--your cares in haste
Rescued the ravag'd realms of Taste;
And LYTTLETON's accomplish'd name,
And witty PULTENEY shar'd the fame;
The Men not bound by pedant rules
Nor Ladies Precieuses ridicules;*
For polish'd WALPOLE show'd the way,
How wits may be both learn'd and gay;
And CARTER taught the female train,
The deeply wise are never vain;
And she who SHAKSPEARE's wrongs redrest,
Prov'd that the brightest are the best.

This just deduction still they drew,
And well they practis'd what they knew;
Nor taste, nor wit, deserves applause,
Unless still true to critic laws;
Good sense, of faculties the best,
Inspire and regulate the rest.
Oh! how unlike the wit that fell,
RAMBOUILLET! at thy quaint Hotel;
Where point, and turn, and equivoque,
Distorted every word they spoke!
All so intolerably bright,
Plain Common Sense was put to flight;
Each speaker, so ingenious ever,
'Twas tiresome to be quite so clever;
There twisted Wit forgot to please,
And Mood and Figure banish'd ease:
No votive altar smok'd to thee,
Chaste Queen, divine Simplicity!
But forc'd Conceit, which ever fails,
And, stff Antithesis prevails;
Uneasy rivalry destroys
Society's unlabour'd joys:
NATURE, of stilts and fetters tir'd,
Impatient from the Wits retir'd;
Long time the Exile houseless stray'd,
Till SEVIGNE receiv'd the maid.
Though here she comes to bless our isle,
Not universal is her smile.
Muse! snatch the Lyre which CAMBRIDGE strung,
When he the empty ballroom sung;
'Tis tun'd above thy pitch, I doubt,
And thou no music wouldst draw out:
Yet, in a lower note, presume
To sing the full dull Drawing-room.
Where the dire Circle keeps its station,
Each common phrase is an oration;
And cracking fans, and whisp'ring Misses,
Compose their Conversation blisses.
The matron marks the goodly show,
While the tall daughter eyes the Beau--
The frigid Beau! Ah! luckless fair,
'Tis not for you that studied air;
Ah! not for you that sidelong glance,
And all that charming nonchalance;
Ah! not for you the three long hours
He worshipp'd the Cosmetic powers;
That finish'd head which breathes perfume,
And kills the nerves of half the room;

And all the murders meant to lie
in that large, languishing, grey eye;
Desist:--less wild th' attempt would be,
To warm the snows of Rhodope:
Too cold to feel, too proud to feign,
For him you're wise and fair in vain;
In vain to charm him you intend,
Self is his object, aim, and end.
Chill shade of that affected Peer,
Who dreaded Mirth, come safely here!
For here no vulgar joy effaces
Thy rage for polish, ton, and graces.
Cold Ceremony's leaden hand
Waves o'er the room her poppy wand;
Arrives the stranger; every guest
Conspires to torture the distrest;
At once they rise--so have I seen--
You guess the simile I mean,
Take what comparison you please,
The crowded streets, the swarming bees,
The pebbles on the shores that lie,
The stars which form the galaxy;
These serve t' embellish what is said,
And show, besides, that one has read;--
At once they rise--th' astonish'd guest
Back in a corner slinks, distrest;
Scar'd at the many bowing round,
And shock'd at her own voice's sound,
Forgot the thing she meant to say,
Her words, half-utter'd, die away;
In sweet oblivion down she sinks,
And of her next appointment thinks.
While her loud neighbour on the right,
Boasts what she has to do to-night;
So very much, you'd swear her pride is
To match the labours of ALCIDES;
'Tis true, in hyperbolic measure,
She nobly calls her labours Pleasure;
In this unlike ALCMENA's son,
She never means they should be done;
Her fancy of no limits dreams,
No ne plus ultra stops her schemes;
Twelve! she'd have scorn'd the paltry round,
No Pillars would have marked her bound;
CALPE and ABYLA, in vain
Had nodded cross th' opposing main;
A circumnavigator she
On Ton's illimitable sea.

We pass the pleasures vast and various.
Of Routs, not social, but gregarious;
Where high heroic self-denial
Sustains her self-inflicted trial.
Day lab'rors! what an easy life,
To feed ten children and a wife!
No--I my juster pity spare
To the night lab'rer's keener care;
And, pleas'd, to gentler scenes retreat,
Where Conversation holds her seat.
Small were that art which would ensure
The Circle's boasted quadrature!
See VESEY's plastic genius make
A Circle every figure take;
Nay, shapes and forms, which would defy
All science of Geometry;
Isoceles, and Parallel,
Names, hard to speak, and hard to spell!
Th' enchantress wav'd her wand, and spoke!
Her potent wand the Circle broke:
The social Spirits hover round,
And bless the liberated ground.
Ask you what charms this gift dispense?
'Tis the strong spell of COMMON SENSE.
Away dull Ceremony flew,
And with her bore Detraction too.
Nor only Geometric Art,
Does this presiding power impart;
But Chemists too, who want the essence,
Which makes or mars all coalescence,
Of her the secret rare might get,
How different kinds amalgamate:
And he, who wilder studies chose,
Find here a new metempsychose;
How forms can other forms assume,
Within her Pythagoric room;
Or be, and stranger is th' event,
The very things which nature meant;
Nor strive, by art and affectation,
To cross their genuine destination.
Here sober Duchesses are seen,
Chaste Wits, and Critics void of spleen;.
Physicians, fraught with real science,
And Whigs and Tories in alliance;
Poets, fulfilling Christian duties,
Just Lawyers, reasonable Beauties;
Bishops who preach, and Peers who pay,
And Countesses who seldom play;

Learn'd Antiquaries, who, from college,
Reject the rust, and bring the knowledge;
And, hear it, age, believe it, youth,
Polemics, really seeking truth;
And Travellers of that rare tribe,
Who've seen the countries they describe;
Who study'd there, so strange their plan,
Not plants, nor herbs alone, but man;
While Travellers, of other notions,
Scale mountain-tops, and traverse oceans;
As if, so much these themes engross,
The study of mankind--was Moss.
Ladies who point, nor think me partial,
An Epigram as well as MARTIAL;
Yet in all female worth succeed,
As well as those who cannot read.
Right pleasant were the task, I ween,
To name the groupes which fill the scene;
But Rhyme's of such fastidious nature,
She proudly scorns all Nomenclature,
Nor grace our Northern names her lips,
Like HOMER's Catalogue of Ships.
Once--faithful Memory! heave a sigh,
Here ROSCIUS gladden'd every eye.
Why comes not MARO? Far from town,
He rears the Urn to Taste, and BROWN;
Plants Cypress round the Tomb of GRAY,
Or decks his English Garden gay;
Whose mingled sweets exhale perfume,
And promise a perennial bloom.
Here, rigid CATO*, awful Sage!
Bold Censor of a thoughtless age,
Once dealt his pointed moral round,
And, not unheeded, fell the sound;
The Muse his honour'd memory weeps,
For CATO now with ROSCIUS sleeps!
Here once HORTENSIUS* lov'd to sit,
Apostate now from social Wit:
Ah! why in wrangling senates waste
The noblest parts, the happiest taste?
Why Democratic Thunders wield,
And quit the Muse's calmer field?
Taste thou the gentler joys they give,
With HORACE, and with LELIUS live.*
Hail, CONVERSATION, soothing Power,
Sweet Goddess of the social hour!
Not with more heart-felt warmth, at least,
Does LELIUS bend, thy true High Priest;

Than I the lowest of thy train,
These field-flowers bring to deck thy fane;
Who to thy shrine like him can haste,
With warmer zeal, or purer taste?
O may thy worship long prevail,
And thy true votaries never fail!
Long may thy polish'd altars blaze
With wax-lights' undiminish'd rays!
Still be thy nightly offerings paid,
Libations large of Lemonade.
On silver vases, loaded, rise
The biscuits' ample sacrifice.
Nor be the milk-white streams forgot
Of thirst-assuaging, cool orgeat;
Rise, incense pure from fragrant Tea,
Delicious incense, worthy Thee!
Hail, Conversation, heav'nly fair,
Thou bliss of life, and balm of care,
Still may thy gentle reign extend,
And taste with wit and science blend!
Soft polisher of rugged man,
Refiner of the social plan;
For thee, best solace of his toil,
The sage consumes his midnight oil;
And keeps late vigils to produce
Materials for thy future use;
Calls forth the else neglected knowledge,
Of school, of travel, and of college.
If none behold, ah! wherefore fair?
Ah! wherefore wise, if none must hear?
Our intellectual ore must shine,
Not slumber idly in the mine.
Let education's moral mint
The noblest images imprint;
Let taste her curious touchstone hold,
To try if standard be the gold;
But 'tis thy commerce, Conversation,
Must give it use by circulation;
That noblest commerce of mankind,
Whose precious merchandize is MIND!
What stoic traveller would try
A sterile soil, and parching sky,
Or dare th' intemperate Northern zone,
If what he saw must ne'er be known?
For this he bids his home farewell;
The joy of seeing is to tell.
Trust me, he never would have stirr'd,
Were he forbid to speak a word;

And Curiosity would sleep,
If her own secrets she must keep
The bliss of telling what is past
Becomes her rich reward at last.
Who'd mock at death, at danger smile,
To steal one peep at Father Nile;
Who, at Palmira, risk his neck,
Or search the ruins of Balbec
If these must hide old Nilus' fount,
Nor Lybian tales at home recount;
If those must sink their learned labour,
Nor with their ruins treat a neighbour?
Range--study--think do all we can
Colloquial pleasures are for man.
Yet not from low desire to shine
Does Genius toil in learning's mine;
Not to indulge in idle vision,
But strike new light by strong collision.
Of CONVERSATION, wisdom's friend,
This is the object and the end,
Of moral truth, man's proper science,
With sense and learning in alliance,
To search the depths, and thence produce
What tends to practice and to use.
And next in value we shall find
What mends the taste and forms the mind.
If high those truths in estimation,
Whose search is crown'd with demonstration;
To these assign no scanty praise,
Our taste which clear, our views which raise.
For grant that mathematic truth
Best balances the mind of Youth;
Yet scarce the truth of Taste is found
To grow from principles less sound.
O'er books the Mind inactive lies,
Books, the Mind's food, not exercise!
Her vigorous wing she scarcely feels,
'Till use latent strength reveals;
Her slumb'ring energies can't forth,
She springs, she mounts, she feels her worth;
And, at her new-found powers elated,
Thinks them not rous'd, but new created.
Enlighten'd spirits! you, who know
What charms from polish'd converse flow,
Speak, for you can, the pure delight
When kindling sympathies unite;
When correspondent tastes impart
Communion sweet from heart to heart;

You ne'er the cold gradations need
Which vulgar souls to union lead;
No dry discussion to unfold
The meaning caught ere well 'tis told:
In taste, in learning, wit, or science,
Still kindred souls demand alliance;
Each in the other joys to find
The image answering to his mind.
But sparks electric only strike
On souls electrical alike;
The flash of intellect expires,
Unless it meet congenial fires:
The language to th' Elect alone
Is, like the Mason's mystery, known;
In vain th' unerring sign is made
To him who is not of the Trade.
What lively pleasure to divine
The thought implied, the hinted line,
To feel Allusion's artful force,
And trace the image to its source.
Quick Memory blends her scatter'd rays,
'Till Fancy kindles at the blaze;
The works of ages start to view,
And ancient Wit elicits new.
But wit and parts if thus we praise,
What nobler altars should we raise.
Those sacrifices could we see
Which wit, O Virtue! makes to thee.
At once the rising thought to dash,
To quench at once the bursting flash!
The shining mischief to subdue,
And lose the praise and pleasure too!
Though Venus' self, could you detect her,
Imbuing with her richest nectar,
The thought unchaste to check that thought,
To spurn a fame so dearly bought,
This is high Principle's controul!
This is true continence of Soul!
Blush, heroes, at your cheap renown,
A vanquish'd realm, a plunder'd town!
Your conquests were to gain a name,
This conquest triumphs over Fame;
So pure its essence, 'twere destroy'd
If known, and if commended, void.
Amidst the brightest truths believ'd,
Amidst the fairest deeds achiev'd,
Shall stand recorded and admir'd,
That Virtue sunk what Wit inspir'd.

But let the letter'd, and the fair,
And, chiefly, let the WIT beware;
You, whose warm spirits never fail,
Forgive the hint which ends my tale:
O shun the perils which attend
On wit, on warmth, and heed your friend.
Though Science nurs'd you in her bowers,
Though Fancy crown your brow with flowers,
Each thought though bright invention fill,
Though Attic bees each word distil;
Yet, if one gracious power refuse
Her gentle influence to infuse;
If she withhold her magic spell,
Nor in the social circle dwell;
In vain shall listening crowds approve,
They'll praise you, but they will not love.
What is this power you're loth to mention,
This charm, this witchcraft? 'tis ATTENTION:
Mute Angel, yes; thy looks dispense
The silence of intelligence;
Thy graceful form I well discern,
In act to listen and to learn;
'Tis thou for talents shalt obtain
That pardon Wit would hope in vain:
Thy wondrous power, thy secret charm,
Shall Envy of her sting disarm;
Thy silent flattery sooths our spirit,
And we forgive eclipsing merit;
Our jealous souls no longer burn,
Nor hate thee, though thou shine in turn;
The sweet atonement screens the fault,
And love and praise are cheaply bought.
With mild complacency to hear,
Though somewhat long the tale appear,
The dull relation to attend,
Which mars the story you could mend;
'Tis more than wit, 'tis moral beauty,
'Tis pleasure rising out of duty.
Nor vainly think the time you waste,
When temper triumphs over taste.

Florio: A Tale, For Fine Gentleman And Fine Ladies. In Two Parts

PART I

Florio, a youth of gay renown,

Who figured much about the town,
Had pass'd, with general approbation,
The modish forms of education;
Knew what was proper to be known,
The establish'd jargon of Bon-ton;
Had learnt, with very moderate reading,
The whole new system of good breeding:
He studied to be cold and rude,
Though native feeling would intrude.
Unlucky sense and sympathy,
Spoilt the vain thing he strove to be:
For Florio was not meant by nature,
A silly, or a worthless creature:
He had a heart disposed to feel,
Had life and spirit, taste and zeal;
Was handsome, generous; but, by fate,
Predestined to a large estate!
Hence, all that graced his opening days,
Was marr'd by pleasure, spoilt by praise.
The Destiny, who wove the thread
Of Florio's being, sigh'd, and said,
'Poor Youth! this cumbrous twist of gold,
More than my shuttle well can hold,
For which thy anxious fathers toil'd,
Thy white and even thread has spoil'd:
'Tis this shall warp thy pliant youth
From sense, simplicity, and truth,
Thy erring sire, by wealth misled,
Shall scatter pleasures round thy head,
When wholesome discipline's control,
Should brace the sinews of thy soul;
Coldly thou'lt toil for learning's prize,
For why should he that's rich be wise?'
The gracious Master of womankind,
Who knew us vain, corrupt, and blind,
In mercy, tho' in anger said,
That man should earn his daily bread;
His lot inaction renders worse,
While labour mitigates the curse.
The idle, life's worst burthens bear,
And meet, what toil escapes, despair.
Forgive, nor lay the fault on me,
This mixture of mythology;
The Muse of Paradise has deign'd
With truth to mingle fables feign'd;
And tho' the Bard who would attain
The glories, Milton, of thy strain,
Will never reach thy style or thoughts,

He may be like thee -- in thy faults.
Exhausted Florio, at the age
When youth should rush on glory's stage;
When life should open fresh and new,
And ardent hope her schemes pursue;
Of youthful gayety bereft,
Had scarce an unbroach'd pleasure left;
He found already to his cost,
The shining gloss of life was lost;
And pleasure was so coy a prude,
She fled the more, the more pursued;
Or if, o'ertaken and caress'd
He loath'd and left her when possess'd.
But Florio knew the World; that science
Sets sense and learning at defiance;
He thought the World to him was known,
Whereas he only knew the Town
In men this blunder still you find,
All think their little set -- Mankind.
Tho' high renown the youth had gain'd,
No flagrant crimes his life had stain'd;
No tool of falsehood, slave of passion,
But spoilt by Custom and the Fashion.
Tho' known among a certain set;
He did not like to be in debt!
He shudder'd at the dicer's box,
Nor thought it very heterodox,
That tradesmen should be sometimes paid,
And bargains kept as well as made.
His growing credit, as a sinner,
Was that he liked to spoil a dinner;
Made pleasure and made business wait,
And still, by system, came too late;
Yet 'twas a hopeful indication,
On which to be found a reputation:
Small habits, well pursued betimes,
May reach the dignity of crimes.
And who a juster claim preferr'd,
Than one who always broke his word?
His mornings were not spent in vice,
'Twas lounging, sauntering, eating ice:
Walk up and down St. James's-Street,
Full fifty times the youth you'd meet:
He hated cards, detested drinking,
But stroll'd to shun the toil of thinking;
'Twas doing nothing was his curse,
Is there a vice can plague us worse?
The wretch who digs the mine for bread,

Or ploughs, that others may be fed,
Feels less fatigue than that decreed
To him who cannot think, or read.
Not all the peril of temptations,
Not all the conflict of the passions,
Can quench the spark of glory's flame,
Or quite extinguish Virtue's name;
Like the true taste for genuine saunter,
Like sloth, the soul's most dire enchanter.
The active fires that stir the breast,
Her poppies charm to fatal rest;
They rule in short and quick succession,
But Sloth keeps one long, fast possession;
Ambition's reign is quickly clos'd,
Th' usurper Rage is soon depos'd;
Intemperance, where there's no temptation,
Makes voluntary abdication;
Of other tyrants short the strife,
But Indolence is king for life.
The despot twists with soft control,
Eternal fetters round the soul.
Yet tho' so polish'd Florio's breeding,
Think him not ignorant of reading;
For he to keep him from the vapours,
Subscrib'd at Hookham's, saw the papers;
Was deep in poet's-corner wit;
Knew what was in Italics writ;
Explain'd fictitious names at will,
Each gutted syllable could fill;
There oft, in paragraphs, his name
Gave symptom sweet of growing fame;
Tho' yet they only serv'd to hint
That Florio lov'd to see in print,
His ample buckles' alter'd shape,
His buttons chang'd, his varying cape.
And many a standard phrase was his
Might rival bore, or banish quiz;
The man who grasps this young renown,
And early starts for fashion's crown;
In time that glorious prize may wield.
Which clubs, and ev'n Newmarket yield.
He studied while he dress'd, for true 'tis,
He read Compendiums, Extracts, Beauties,
Abreges, Dictionaires, Recueils,
Mercures, Journaux, Extraits, and Feuilles:
No work in substance now is follow'd,
The Chemic Extract only 's swallow'd.
He lik'd those literary cooks

Who skim the cream of others' books;
And ruin half an Author's graces,
By plucking bon-mots from their places;
He wonders any writing sells,
But these spic'd mushrooms and morells;
His palate these alone can touch,
Where every mouthful is bonne bouche.
Some phrase, that with the public took,
Was all he read of any book;
For plan, detail, arrangement, system,
He let them go, and never miss'd 'em.
Of each new Play he saw a part,
And all the Anas had my heart;
He found whatever they produce
Is fit for conversation-use;
Learning so ready for display,
A page would prime him for a day:
They cram not with a mass of knowledge,
Which smacks of toil, and smells of college,
Which in the memory useless lies,
Or only makes men -- good and wise.
This might have merit once indeed,
But now for other ends we read.
A friend he had, Bellario hight,
A reasoning, reading, learned wight;
At least, with men of Florio's breeding,
He was a prodigy of reading.
He knew each stale and vapid lie
In tomes of French Philosophy;
And then, we fairly may presume,
From Pyrrho down to David Hume,
'Twere difficult to single out
A man more full of shallow doubt;
He knew the little sceptic prattle,
The sophist's paltry arts of battle;
Talk'd gravely of the Atomic dance,
Of moral fitness, fate, and chance;
Admired the system of Lucretius,
Whose matchless verse makes nonsense specious!
To this his doctrine owes its merits,
Like poisonous reptiles kept in spirits.
Though sceptics dull his schemes rehearse,
Who have not souls to taste his verse.
Bellario founds his reputation
On dry, stale jokes, about Creation;
Would prove, by argument circuitous,
The combination was fortuitous.
Swore Priests' whole trade was to deceive,

And prey on bigots who believe;
With bitter ridicule could jeer,
And had the true free-thinking jeer.
Grave arguments he had in store,
Which have been answer'd o'er and o'er;
And used, with wondrous penetration
The trite old trick of false citation;
From ancient Authors fond to quote
A phrase or thought they never wrote.
Upon his highest shelf there stood
The Classics neatly cut in wood;
And in a more commodious station,
You'd found them in a French translation:
He swears, 'tis from the Greek he quotes,
But keeps the French -- just for the notes.
He worshipp'd certain modern names
Who History write in Epigrams,
In pointed periods, shining phrases,
And all the small poetic daisies,
Which crowd the pert and florid style,
Where fact is dropt to raise a smile;
Where notes indecent or profane
Serve to raise doubts, but not explain:
Where all is spangle, glitter, show,
And truth is overlaid below:
Arts scorn'd by History's sober muse
Arts Clarendon disdain'd to use.
Whate'er the subject of debate,
'Twas larded still with sceptic prate;
Begin whatever theme you will,
In unbelief he lands you still;
The good, with shame I speak it, feel
Not half this proselyting zeal;
While cold their Master's cause to own
Content to go to Heaven alone;
The infidel in liberal trim,
Would carry all the World with him;
Would treat his wife, friend, kindred, nation,
Mankind -- with what? -- Annihilation.
Though Florio did not quite believe him,
He thought, why should a friend deceive him?
Much as he prized Bellario's wit,
He liked not all his notions yet;
He thought him charming, pleasant, odd,
But hoped one might believe in God;
Yet such the charms that graced his tongue,
He knew not how to think him wrong.
Though Florio tried a thousand ways,

Truth's insuppressive torch would blaze;
Where once her flame was burnt, I doubt
If ever it go fairly out.
Yet, under great Bellario's care,
He gain'd each day a better air;
With many a leader of renown,
Deep in the learning of the Town,
Who never other science knew,
But what from that prime source they drew;
Pleased to the Opera, they repair,
To get recruits of knowledge there,
Mythology gain at a glance,
And learn the Classics from a dance:
In Ovid they ne'er cared a groat,
How fared the venturous Argonaut;
Yet charm'd they see Medea rise
On fiery dragons to the skies.
For Dido, though they never knew her
As Maro's magic pencil drew her,
Faithful and fond, and broken-hearted,
Her pious vagabond departed;
Yet, for Didone how they roar!
And Cara! Cara! loud encore.
One taste, Bellario's soul possess'd,
The master passion of his breast;
It was not one of those frail joys,
Which, by possession, quickly cloys;
This bliss was solid, constant, true;
'Twas action, and 'twas passion too;
For though the business might be finish'd,
The pleasure scarcely was diminish'd;
Did he ride out, or sit, or walk?
He lived it o'er again in talk;
Prolong'd the fugitive delight,
In words by day, in dreams by night.
'Twas eating did his soul allure,
A deep, keen, modish Epicure;
Though once his name, as I opine,
Meant not such men as live to dine.
Yet all our modern Wits assure us,
That's all they know of Epicurus:
They fondly fancy, that repletion
Was the chief good of that famed Grecian.
To live in gardens full of flowers,
And talk philosophy in bowers.
Or, in the covert of a wood,
To descant on the sovereign good,
Might be the notion of their founder,

But they have notions vastly sounder;
Their bolder standards they erect,
To form a more substantial sect;
Old Epicurus would not own 'em,
A dinner is their summum bonum.
More like you'll find such sparks as these
To Epicurus' deities;
Like them they mix not with affairs,
But loll and laugh at human cares,
To beaux this difference is allow'd,
They choose a sofa for a cloud;
Bellario had embraced with glee,
This practical philosophy.
Young Florio's father had a friend,
And ne'er did Heaven a worthier send;
A cheerful knight of good estate,
Whose heart was warm, whose bounty great.
Where'er his wide protection spread,
The sick were cheer'd the hungry fed;
Resentment vanish'd where he came,
And law-suits fled before his name:
The old esteem'd, the young caress'd him,
And all the smiling village bless'd him.
Within his castle's Gothic gate,
Sate plenty, and old-fashion'd State:
Scarce Prudence could his bounties stint;
Such characters are out of print;
O! would kind Heaven, the age to mend,
A new edition of them send,
Before our tottering Castles fall,
And swarming Nabobs seize on all!
Some little whims he had, 'tis true,
But they were harmless, and were few;
He dreaded nought like alteration,
Improvement still was innovation;
He said, when any change was brewing,
Reform was a fine name for ruin;
This maxim firmly he would hold,
'That always must be good that's old.'
The acts which dignify the day
He thought portended its decay:
And fear'd 'twould show a falling State,
If Sternhold should give way to Tate:
The Church's downfal he predicted,
Were modern tunes not interdicted;
He scorn'd them all, but crown'd with palm
The man who set the hundredth Psalm.
Of moderate parts, of moderate wit,

But parts for life and business fit,
Whate'er the theme, he did not fail,
At Popery and the French to rail;
And started wide, with fond digression,
To praise the Protestant succession;
Of Blackstone he had read a part,
And all Burns' Justice knew by heart.
He thought man's life too short to waste
On idle things call'd wit and taste.
In books that he might lose no minute,
His very verse had business in it.
He ne'er had heard of Bards of Greece,
But had read half of Dyer's Fleece.
His sphere of knowledge still was wider,
His Georgics, 'Philips upon Cyder;'
He could produce in proper place,
Three apt quotations from the 'Chace,'
Ad in the hall from day to day,
Old Isaac Walton's Angler lay.
This good and venerable knight,
One daughter had, his soul's delight;
For face, no mortal could resist her,
She smiled like Hebe's youngest sister;
Her life, as lovely as her face,
Each duty mark'd with every grace;
Her native sense improved by reading,
Her native sweetness by good-breeding:
She had perused each choicer sage
Of ancient date, or later age;
But her best knowledge still she found
On sacred, not on Classic ground;
'Twas thence her noblest stores she drew,
And well she practised what she knew.
Let by Simplicity divine,
She pleased, and never tried to shine;
She gave to chance each unschool'd feature,
And left her cause to sense and Nature.
The Sire of Florio, ere he died,
Decreed fair Celia Florio's bride;
Bade him his latest wish attend,
And win the daughter of his friend;
When the last rites to him were paid,
He charged him to address the maid;
Sir Gilbert's heart the wish approved,
For much his ancient friend he loved.
Six rapid months like lightning fly,
And the last gray was now thrown by;
Florio, reluctant, calls to mind

The orders of a Sire too kind;
Yet go he must; he must fulfil
The hard conditions of the will:
Go, at that precious hour of prime,
Go, at that swarming, bustling time,
When the full town to joy invites,
Distracted with its own delights;
When pleasure pours from her full urn,
Each tiresome transport in its turn;
When Dissipation's altars blaze,
And men run mad a thousand ways;
When, on his tablets, there were found
Engagements for full six weeks round;
Must leave, with grief and desperation,
Three packs of cards of invitation,
And all the ravishing delights
Of slavish days, and sleepless nights.
Ye nymphs, whom tyrant Power drags down,
With hand despotic, from the town,
When Almack's doors wide open stand,
And the gay partner's offer'd hand
Courts to the dance; when steaming rooms
Fetid with unguents and perfumes,
Invite you to the mobs polite
Of three sure balls in one short night;
You may conceive what Florio felt,
And sympathetically melt;
You may conceive the hardship dire,
To lawns and woodlands to retire,
When freed from Winter's icy chain,
Glad Nature revels on the plain;
When blushing Spring leads on the hours,
And May is prodigal of flowers;
When Passion warbles through the grove,
And all is song, and all is love;
When new-born breezes sweep the vale,
And health adds fragrance to the vale.

PART II

Six boys, unconscious of their weight,
Soon lodged him at Sir Gilbert's gate;
His trusty Swiss, who flew still faster,
Announced the arrival of his Master:
So loud the rap which shook the door,
The hall re-echoed to the roar;
Since first the castle walls were rear'd,

So dread a sound had ne'er been heard;
The din alarm'd the frighten'd deer
Who in a corner slunk for fear,
The Butler thought 'twas beat of drum,
The Steward swore the French were come;
It ting'd with red Poor Florio's face,
He thought himself in Portland-Place.
Short joy! he enter'd, and the gate
Closed on him with its ponderous weight.
Who, like Sir Gilbert, now was blest?
With rapture he embraced his guest.
Fair Celia blush'd, and Florio utter'd
Half sentences, or rather mutter'd
Disjointed words -- as, 'honour! pleasure!
'Kind! -- vastly good, Ma'am! -- beyond measure:'
Tame expletives, with which dull Fashion
Fills vacancies of sense and passion.
Yet, though disciple of cold Art,
Florio soon found he had a heart,
He saw; and but that Admiration
Had been too active, too like passion;
Or had he been to Ton less true,
Cupid had shot him through and through;
But, vainly speeds the surest dart,
Where Fashion's mail defends the heart
The shaft her cold repulsion found,
And fell, without the power to wound;
For fashion, with a mother's joy,
Dipp'd in her lake the darling boy;
That lake whose chilling waves impart
The gift to freeze the warmest heart:
Yet guarded as he was with phlegm,
With such delight he eyed the dame,
Found his cold heart so melt before her,
And felt so ready to adore her;
That fashion fear'd her son would yield,
And flew to snatch him from the field;
O'er his touch'd heart her AEgis threw,
The Goddess Mother straight he knew;
Her power he own'd, she saw and smiled,
And claim'd the triumph of her child.
Celia a table still supplied,
Which modish luxury might deride;
A modest feast the hope conveys,
The Master eats on other days;
While gorgeous banquets oft bespeak
A hungry household all the week;
And decent elegance was there,

And Plenty with her liberal air.
But vulgar Plenty gave offence,
And shock'd poor Florio's nicer sense.
Patient he yielded to his fate,
When good Sir Gilbert piled his plate;
He bow'd submissive, made no question,
But that 'twas sovereign for digestion;
But, such was his unlucky whim,
Plain meats would ne'er agree with him;
Yet feign'd to praise the gothic treat,
And, if he ate not, seem'd to eat.
In sleep sad Florio hoped to find,
The pleasures he had left behind,
He dreamt, and, lo! to charm his eyes,
The form of Weltje seem'd to rise;
The gracious vision waved his wand,
And banquets sprung to Florio's hand;
Th' imaginary savours rose
In tempting odours to his nose.
A bell, not Fancy's false creation,
Gives joyful 'note of preparation;'
He starts, he wakes, the bell he hears;
Alas! it rings for morning prayers.
But how to spend next tedious morning,
Was past his possible discerning;
Unable to amuse himself,
He tumbled every well-ranged shelf;
This book was dull, and that was wise,
And this was monstrous as to size.
With eager joy he gobbled down
Whate'er related to the town;
Whate'er look'd small, whate'er look'd new,
Half-bound, or stitch'd in pink or blue;
Old play-bills, Astley's last year's feats,
And Opera disputes in sheets,
As these dear records meet his eyes,
Ghosts of departed pleasures rise;
He lays the book upon the shelf,
And leaves the day to spend itself.
To cheat the tedious hours, whene'er
He sallied forth to take the air,
His sympathetic ponies knew
Which way their Lord's affections drew;
And, every time he went abroad,
Sought of themselves the London road:
He ask'd each mile of every clown,
How far they reckon'd it to town?
And still his nimble spirits rise,

Whilst thither he directs his eyes;
But when his coursers back he guides,
The sinking Mercury quick subsides.
A week he had resolved to stay,
But found a week in every day;
Yet if the gentle maid was by,
Faint pleasure glisten'd in his eye;
Whene'er she spoke, attention hung
On the mild accents of her tongue;
But when no more the room she graced,
The slight impression was effaced.
Whene'er Sir Gilbert's sporting guests
Retail'd old news, or older jests,
Florio, quite calm, and debonair,
Still humm'd a new Italian air;
He did not even feign to hear them,
But plainly show'd he could not bear them.
Celia perceived his secret thoughts,
But liked the youth with all his thoughts,
Yet 'twas unlike, she softly said,
The tales of love which she had read,
Where heroes vow'd, and sigh'd, and knelt;
Nay, 'twas unlike the love she felt;
Though when her Sire the youth would blame,
She clear'd his but suspected fame,
Ventured to hope, with faultering tongue,
'He would reform, he was but young;'
Confess'd his manners wrong in part,
'But then -- he had so good a heart!'
She sunk each fault, each virtue raised,
And still, where truth permitted, praised;
His interest farther to secure,
She praised his bounty to the poor;
For, votary as his he was of art,
He had a kind and melting heart;
Though, with a smile, he used to own
He had not time to feel in town;
Not that he blush'd to show compassion,--
It chanced that year to be the fashion.
And equally the modish tribe,
To Clubs or Hospitals subscribe.
At length, to wake Ambition's flame,
A letter from Bellario came;
Announcing the supreme delight,
Preparing for a certain night,
By Flavia fair, return'd from France,
Who took him captive at a glance:
The invitations all were given!

Five hundred cards! -- a little heaven!--
A dinner first -- he would present him,
And nothing, nothing must prevent him.
Whosever wish'd a noble air,
Must gain it by an entree there;
Of all the glories of the town,
'Twas the first passport to renown.
Then ridiculed his rural schemes,
His pastoral shades, and purling streams;
Sneer'd at his present brilliant life,
His polish'd Sire, and high-bred Wife!
Thus doubly to inflame, he tried,
His curiosity, and pride.
The youth, with agitated heart,
Prepared directly to depart;
But, bound in honour to obey
His father, at no distant day,
He promised soon to hasten down,
Though business call'd him now to town;
Then faintly hints a cold proposal--
But leaves it to the Knight's disposal--
Stammer'd half words of love and duty,
And mutter'd much of -- 'worth and beauty;'
Something of 'passion' then he dropt,
'And hoped his ardour'-- Here he stopt;
For some remains of native truth
Flush'd in his face, and check'd the youth;
Yet still the ambiguous suffusion,
Might pass for artless love's confusion.
The doating father thought 'twas strange,
But fancied men like times might change;
Yet own'd, nor could he check his tongue,
It was not so when he was young.
That was the reign of Love, he swore,
Whose halcyon days are now no more.
In that bless'd age, for honour famed,
Love paid the homage Virtue claim'd;
Not that insipid, daudling Cupid,
With heart so hard, and air so stupid,
Who coldly courts the charms which lie
In Affectation's half closed eye.
Love then was honest, genuine passion,
And manly gallantry the fashion;
Yet pure as ardent was the flame
Excited by the beauteous dame;
Hope should subsist on slender bounties,
And Suitors gallop'd o'er two counties,
The Ball's fair partner to behold,

Or humbly hope -- she caught no cold.
But mark how much Love's annals mend!
Should Beauty's Goddess now descend;
On some adventure should she come,
To grace a modish drawing-room;
Spite of her form and heavenly air,
What Beau would hand her to her chair?
Vain were that grace, which, to her son,
Disclosed what Beauty had not done:
Vain were that motion which betray'd,
The goddess was no earth-born maid;
If noxious Faro's baleful spright,
With rites infernal ruled the night,
The group absorb'd in play and pelf,
Venus might call her doves herself.
As Florio pass'd the Castle-gate,
His spirits seem to lose their weight;
He feasts his lately vacant mind
With all the joys he hopes to find;
Yet on whate'er his fancy broods,
The form of Celia still intrudes;
Whatever other sounds he hears,
The voice of Celia fills his ears;
Howe'er his random thoughts might fly,
Nor was the obstrusive vision o'er,
Even when he reach'd Bellario's door;
The friends embraced with warm delight,
And Flavia's praises crown'd the night.
Soon dawn'd the day which was to show
Glad Florio what was heaven below.
Flavia, admired wherever known,
The acknowledged Empress of bon-ton;
O'er Fashion's wayward kingdom reigns,
And holds Bellario in her chains:
Various her powers; a wit by day,
By night unmatch'd for lucky play.
The flattering, fashionable tribe,
Each stray bon-mot to her ascribe;
And all her 'little senate' own
She made the best Charade in town;
Her midnight suppers always drew
Whate'er was fine, whate'er was new.
There oft the brightest fame you'd see
The victim of a repartee;
For slander's Priestess still supplies
The Spotless for the sacrifice.
None at her polish'd table sit,
But who aspired to modish wit;

The persiflage, th' unfeeling jeer,
The civil, grave, ironic sneer;
The laugh, which more than censure wounds,
Which, more than argument, confounds.
There the fair deed, which would engage
The wonder of a nobler age,
With unbelieving scorn is heard,
Or still to selfish ends referr'd;
If in the deed no flaw they find,
To some base motive 'tis assign'd;
When Malice longs to throw her dart,
But finds no vulnerable part,
Because the Virtues all defend,
At every pass, their guarded friend;
Then by one slight insinuation,
One scarce perceived exaggeration;
Sly Ridicule, with half a word,
Can fix her stigma of -- absurd;
Nor care, nor skill, extracts the dart,
With which she stabs the feeling heart;
Her cruel caustics inly pain,
And scars indelible remain.
Supreme in wit, supreme in play,
Despotic Flavia all obey;
Small were her natural charms of face,
Till heighten'd with each foreign grace;
But what subdued Bellario's soul
Beyond Philosophy's control,
Her constant table was as fine
As if ten Rajahs were to dine;
She every day produced such fish as
Would gratify the nice Apicius,
Or realize what we think fabulous
I' th' bill of fare of Heliogabalus.
Yet still the natural taste was cheated,
'Twas deluged in some sauce one hated.
'Twas sauce! 'twas sweetmeat! 'twas confection!
All poignancy! and all perfection!
Rich Entrements, whose name none knows,
Ragouts, Tourtes, Tendrons, Fricandeaux,
Might picque the sensuality
O' th' hogs of Epicurus' sty;
Yet all so foreign, and so fine,
'Twas easier to admire, than dine.
O! if the Muse had power to tell
Each dish, no Muse has power to spell!
Great Goddess of the French Cuisine!
Not with unhallow'd hands I mean

To violate thy secret shade,
Which eyes profane shall ne'er invade;
No! of thy dignity supreme,
I, with 'mysterious reverence,' deem!
Or, should I venture with rash hand,
The vulgar would not understand;
None but th' initiated know
The raptures keen thy rites bestow.
Thus much to tell I lawful deem,
Thy works are never what they seem;
Thy will this general law has past,
That nothing of itself shall taste.
Thy word this high decree enacted,
'In all be Nature counteracted!'
Conceive, who can, the perfect bliss,
For 'tis not given to all to guess,
The rapturous joy Bellario found,
When thus his every wish was crown'd.
To Florio, as the best of friends,
One dish he secretly commends;
Then hinted, as a special favour,
What gave it that delicious flavour;
A mystery he so much reveres,
He never to unhallow'd ears
Would trust it, but to him would show
How far true Friendship's power could go.
Florio, though dazzled by the fete,
With far inferior transport eat;
A little warp his taste had gain'd,
Which, unperceived, till now, remain'd;
For, from himself he would conceal
The change he did not choose to feel;
He almost wish'd he could be picking
An unsophisticated chicken;
And when he cast his eyes around,
And not one simple morsel found,
O give me, was his secret wish,
My charming Celia's plainest dish!
Thus Nature, struggling for her rights,
Lets in some little, casual lights,
And Love combines to war with Fashion,
Though yet 'twas but an infant passion;
The practised Flavia tried each art
Of sly attack to steal his heart;
Her forced civilities oppress,
Fatiguing through mere graciousness;
While many a gay, intrepid dame,
By bold assault essay'd the same.

Fill'd with disgust, he strove to fly
The artful glance and fearless eye;
Their jargon now no more he praises,
Nor echoes back their flimsy phrases.
He felt not Celia's powers of face,
Till weigh'd against bon-ton grimage;
Nor half her genuine beauties tasted,
Till with factitious charms contrasted.
Th' industrious harpies hover'd round,
Nor peace nor liberty he found;
By force and flattery circumvented,
To play, reluctant, he consented;
Each Dame her power of pleasing tried,
To fix the novice by her side;
Of Pigeons, he the very best,
Who wealth, with ignorance, possest:
But Flavia's rhetoric best persuades,
That Sibyl leads him to the shades;
The fatal leaves around the room,
Prophetic, tell th' approaching doom!
Yet, different from the tale of old,
It was the fair one pluck'd the gold;
Her arts the ponderous purse exhaust;
A thousand borrow'd, staked, and lost,
Wakes him to sense and shame again,
Nor force, nor fraud, could more obtain.
He rose, indignant, to attend
The summons of a ruin'd friend,
Whom keen Bellario's arts betray
To all the depths of desperate play;
A thoughtless youth who near him sate,
Was plunder'd of his whole estate;
Toll late he call'd for Florio's aid,
A beggar in a moment made.
And now, with horror, Florio views
The wild confusion which ensues;
Marks how the Dames, of late so fair,
Assume a fierce demoniac air;
Marks where th' infernal furies hold
Their orgies foul o'er heaps of gold;
And spirits dire appear to rise,
Guarding the horrid mysteries;
Marks how deforming passions tear
The bosoms of the losing fair;
How looks convulsed, and haggar'd faces
Chase the scared Loves and frighten'd Graces!
Touch'd with disdain, with horror fired,
Celia! he murmur'd, and retired.

That night no sleep his eyelids prest,
He thought; and thought 's a foe to rest:
Or if, by chance, he closed his eyes,
What hideous spectres round him rise!
Distemper'd Fancy wildly brings
The broken images of things;
His ruin'd friend, with eye-ball fixt,
Swallowing the draught Despair had mixt;
The frantic wife beside him stands,
With bursting heart, and wringing hands;
And every horror dreams bestow,
Of pining Want, or raving Woe.
Next morn, to check, or cherish thought,
His library's retreat he sought;
He view'd each book, with cold regard,
Of serious sage, or lighter bard;
At length among the motley band,
The Idler fell into his hand;
Th' alluring title caught his eye,
It promised cold inanity:
He read with rapture and surprise,
And found 'twas pleasant, though 'twas wise;
His tea grew cold, whilst he, unheeding,
Pursued this reasonable reading.
He wonder'd at the change he found,
Th' elastic spirits nimbly bound;
Time slipt, without disgust, away,
While many a card unanswer'd lay;
Three papers, reeking from the press,
Three Pamphlets thin, in azure dress,
Ephemeral literature well known,
The lie and scandal of the town;
Poison of letters, morals, time!
Assassin of our day's fresh prime!
These, on his table, half the day,
Unthought of, and neglected lay.
Florio had now full three hours read,
Hours which he used to waste in bed;
His pulse beat Virtue's vigorous tone,
The reason to himself unknown;
And if he stopp'd to seek the cause,
Fair Celia's image fill'd the pause.
And now, announced, Bellario's name
Had almost quench'd the new-born flame:
'Admit him,' was the ready word
Which first escaped him not unheard;
When sudden to his mental sight,
Uprose the horrors of last night;

His plunder'd friend before him stands,
And -- 'not at home,' his firm commands.
He felt the conquest as a joy
The first temptation would destroy.
He knew next day that Hymen's hand,
Would tack the slight and slippery band,
Which, in loose bondage, would ensnare
Bellario bright and Flavia fair.
Oft had he promised to attend
The Nuptials of his happy friend:
To go -- to stay -- alike he fears;
At length a bolder flight he dares;
To Celia he resolves to fly,
And catch fresh virtue from her eye;
Though three full weeks did yet remain,
Ere he engaged to come again.
This plan he tremblingly embraced,
With doubtful zeal, and uttering haste;
Nor ventured he one card to read,
Which might his virtuous scheme impede;
Each note, he dreaded might betray him,
And shudder'd lest each rap should stay him.
Behold him seated in his chaise:
With face that self-distrust betrays;
He hazards not a single glance,
Nor through the glasses peeps by chance,
Lest some old friend, or haunt well known,
Should melt his resolution down.
Fast as his foaming coursers fly,
Hyde-Park attracts his half-raised eye;
He steals one fearful, conscious look,
Then drops his eye upon his book.
Triumphant he persists to go;
But gives one sigh to Rotten Row.
Long as he view'd Augusta's towers
The sight relax'd his thinking powers;
In vain he better plans revolves,
While the soft scene his soul dissolves;
The towers once lost, his view he bends,
Where the receding smoke ascends;
But when nor smoke, nor towers arise,
To charm his heart or cheat his eyes;
When once he got entirely clear
From this enfeebling atmosphere;
His mind was braced, his spirits light,
His heart was gay, his humour bright;
Thus feeling, at his inmost soul,
The sweet reward of self-control.

Impatient now, and all alive,
He thought he never should arrive;
At last he spies Sir Gilbert's trees;
Now the near battlements he sees;
The gates he enter'd with delight,
And, self-announced, embraced the knight:
The youth his joy unfeign'd express'd,
The knight with joy received his guest,
And own'd, with no unwilling tongue,
'Twas done like men when he was young.
Three weeks subducted, went to prove,
A feeling like old-fashion'd love.
For Celia, not a word she said,
But blush'd, 'celestial, rosy red!'
Her modest charms transport the youth,
Who promised everlasting truth.
Celia, in honour of the day,
Unusual splendour would display:
Such was the charm her sweetness gave,
He thought her Wedgwood had been seve;
Her taste diffused a gracious air,
And chaste Simplicity was there,
Whose secret power, though silent, great is,
The loveliest of the sweet Penates.
Florio, now present to the scene,
With spirits light and gracious mien,
Sir Gilbert's port politely praises,
And carefully avoids French phrases;
Endures the daily dissertation
On Land-tax, and a ruin'd Nation;
Listens to many a tedious tale
Of poachers, who deserved a jail;
Heard of all the business of the Quorum,
Each cause and crime produced before 'em;
Heard them abuse with complaisance
The language, wines, and wits of France;
Nor did he hum a single air,
While good Sir Gilbert fill'd his chair.
Abroad, with joy and grateful pride
He walks, with Celia by his side:
A thousand cheerful thoughts arise,
Each rural scene enchants his eyes:
With transport he begins to look
On Nature's all-instructive book;
No objects now seem mean, or low,
Which point to Him from whom they flow.
A berry or a bud excites
A chain of reasoning which delights,

Which, spite of sceptic ebullitions
Proves Atheists not the best Logicians.
A tree, a brook, a blade of grass,
Suggests reflections as they pass,
Till Florio, with a sigh, confest
The simplest pleasures are the best!
Bellario's systems sink in air,
He feels the perfect, good, and fair.
As pious Celia raised the theme
To holy faith and love supreme;
Enlighten'd Florio learn'd to trace
In Nature's God the God of Grace.
In wisdom as the convert grew,
The hours on rapid pinions flew;
When call'd to dress, that Titus wore
A wig the alter'd Florio swore;
Or else, in estimating time,
He ne'er had mark'd it as a crime,
That he had lost but one day's blessing,
When we so many lose, by dressing.
The rest, suffice it now to say,
Was finish'd in the usual way.
Cupid impatient for his hour,
Reviled slow Themis' tedious power,
Whose parchment legends, signing, sealing,
Are cruel forms for Love to deal in.
At length to Florio's eager eyes,
Behold the day of bliss arise!
The golden sun illumes the globe,
The burning torch, the saffron robe,
Jus as of old, glad Hymen wears,
And Cupid as of old, appears
In Hymen's train; so strange the case,
They hardly knew each other's face;
Yet both confess'd with glowing heart,
They never were design'd to part;
Quoth Hymen, Sure you're strangely slighted,
At weddings not to be invited;
The reason's clear enough, quoth Cupid,
My company is thought but stupid,
Where Plutus is the favourite guest,
For he and I scarce speak at best.
The self-same sun which joins the twain
Sees Flavia sever'd from her swain:
Bellario sues for a divorce,
And both pursue their separate course.
Oh wedded love; Thy bliss how rare!
And yet the ill-assorted pair,

The pair who choose at Fashion's voice,
Or drag the chain of venal choice,
Have little cause to curse the state;
Who make, should never blame their fate;
Such flimsy ties, say where's the wonder,
If Doctors Commons snap asunder.
In either case, 'tis still the wife,
Gives cast and colour to the life.
Florio escaped from Fashion's school,
His heart and conduct learns to rule;
Conscience his useful life approves;
He serves his God, his country loves;
Reveres her laws, protects her rights,
And, for her interests, pleads or fights:
Reviews with scorn his former life,
And, for his rescue, thanks his Wife.

Humble and Unnoticed Virtue

O my son!
The ostentatious virtues which still press
For notice and for praise; the brilliant deeds
Which live but in the eye of observation -
These have their meed at once; but there's a joy
To the fond votaries of fame unknown, -
To hear the still small voice of conscience speak
Its whispering plaudit to the silent soul.
Heaven notes the sigh afflicted goodness heaves,
Hears the low plaint by human ear unheard,
And, from the cheek of patient sorrow, wipes
The tear, by mortal eye unseen, or scorn'd.

The True Heroes: Or, The Noble Army Of Martyrs

You who love a tale of glory,
Listen to the song I sing:
Heroes of the Christian story
Are the heroes I shall bring.

Warriors of the world, avaunt!
Other heroes me engage;
'Tis not such as you I want,
Saints and Martyrs grace my page.

Warriors who the world o'ercame
Were in brother's blood imbrued;
While the saints of purer fame,
Greater far themselves subdued.

Fearful Christian! hear with wonder,
Of the Saints of whom I tell;
Some were burnt, some sawn asunder,
Some by fire or torture fell;

Some to savage beasts were hurl'd,
One escaped the lion's den;
Was a persecuting world
Worthy of these wondrous men?

Some in fiery furnace thrown,
Yet escaped, unsinged their hair;
There Almighty power was shown,
For the Son of God was there.

Let us crown with deathless fame
Those who scorn'd and hated fell;
Martyrs met contempt and shame,
Fearing nought but sin and hell.

How the shower of stones descended,
Holy Stephen, on thy head!
While his tongue the truth defended,
How the glorious Martyr bled!

See his fierce reviler Saul,
How he rails with impious breath!
Then observe converted Paul
Oft in perils, oft in death.

'Twas that God, whose sovereign power
Did the lion's fury 'suage,
Could alone, in one short hour,
Still the persecutor's rage.

E'en a woman - women hear,
Read in Maccabees the story,
Conquer'd nature, love, and fear,
To obtain a crown of glory.

Seven stout sons she saw expire,
(How the mother's soul was pain'd!)
Some by sword, and some by fire,

(How the Martyr was sustain'd!)

E'en in death's acutest anguish
Each the tyrant still defy'd;
Each she saw in torture languish,
Last of all the mother died.

Martyrs who were thus arrested,
In their short but bright career,
By their blood the truth attested,
Proved their faith and love sincere.

Though their lot was hard and lowly,
Though they perish'd at the stake,
Now they live with Christ in glory,
Since they suffer'd for his sake.

Fierce and unbelieving foes
But their bodies could destroy;
Short, though bitter were their woes,
Everlasting is their joy.

On C. Dicey, Esq., In Claybrook Church, Leicestershire

O Thou, or friend or stranger, who shalt tread
These solemn mansions of the silent dead!
Think, when this record to enquiring eyes,
No more shall tell the spot where Dicey lies;
When this frail marble, faithless to its trust,
Mould'ring itself, resigns its moulder'd dust;
When time shall fail, and nature's self decay;
And earth, and sun, and skies dissolve away;

Thy soul, this consummation shall survive,
Defy the wreck, and but begin to live.
This truth, long slighted, let these ashes teach,
Tho' cold, instruct you, and tho' silent, preach:
O pause! reflect, repent, resolve, amend!
Life has no length, Eternity no end!

The Impossibility Conquered: Or, Love Your Neighbour As Yourself

In the Manner of Sir Walter Raleigh

The Objector

Each man who lives, the Scriptures prove,
Must as himself his neighbour love;
But though the precept's full of beauty,
'Tis an impracticable duty:
I'll prove how hard it is to find
A lover of this wondrous kind.

Who loves himself to great excess,
You'll grant must love his neighbour less;
When self engrosses all the heart
How can another have a part?
Then if self-love most men enthrall,
A neighbour's share is none at all.

Say, can the man who hoards up pelf
E'er love his neighbour as himself?
For if he did, would he not labour
To hoard a little for his neighbour?
Then tell me, friend, can hoarding elves
E'er love their neighbour as themselves?

The man whose heart is bent on pleasure
Small love will to his neighbour measure:
Who solely studies his own good,
Can't love another if he would.
Then how can pleasure-hunting elves
E'er love their neighbour as themselves?

Can he whom sloth and loitering please
E'er love his neighbour like his ease ?
Or he who feels ambition's flame
Loves he his neighbour like his fame ?
Such lazy, or such soaring elves
Can't love their neighbour as themselves.

He, whose gross appetites enslave him,
Who spends or feasts the wealth God gave him;
Full pamper'd, gorged at every meal,
He cannot for the empty feel.
How can such gormandizing elves
E'er love their neighbour as themselves?

Then since the man who lusts for gold,
Since he who is to pleasure sold;
Who soars in pride, or sinks in ease,
His neighbour will not serve or please;
Where shall we hope the man to find

To fill this great command inclined?

I dare not blame God's holy word,
Nor censure Scripture as absurd;
But sure the rule's of no avail
If placed so high that all must fail;
And 'tis impossible to prove
That any can his neighbour love.

The Answerer
Yes, such there are of heavenly mould,
Unwarp'd by pleasure, ease, or gold,
He who fulfils the nobler part
By loving God with all his heart;
He, only he, the Scriptures prove,
Can, as himself, his neighbour love.

Then join, to make a perfect plan,
The love of God to love of Man;
Your heart in union both must bring,
This is the stream, and that the spring;
This done, no more in vain you'll labour,
A Christian can't but love his neighbour.

If then the rule's too hard to please ye,
Turn Christian, and you'll find it easy.
'Still 'tis impossible,' you cry,
'In vain shall feeble nature try.'
'Tis true; but know a Christian is a creature,
Who does things quite impossible to nature.

A Christmas Hymn

O now wondrous is the story
Of our blest Redeemer's birth?
See the mighty Lord of Glory
Leaves his heaven to visit earth!

Hear with transport, every creature,
Hear the Gospel's joyful sound;
Christ appears in human nature,
In our sinful world is found;

Comes to pardon our transgression,
Like a cloud our sins to blot;
Comes to his own favour'd nation,

But his own receive him not.

If the angels who attended
To declare the Saviour's birth,
Who from heaven with songs descended
To proclaim good-will on earth:

If, in pity to our blindness,
They had brought the pardon needed,
Still Jehovah's wondrous kindness
Had our warmest hopes exceeded.

If some prophet had been sent
With Salvation's joyful news,
Who that heard the blest event
Could their warmest love refuse?

But 'twas he to whom in Heaven
Hallelujahs never cease;
He, the mighty God, was given,
Given to us a Prince of Peace.

None but he who did create us
Could redeem from sin and hell;
None but he could reinstate us
In the rank from which we fell.

Had he come, the glorious stranger,
Deck'd with all the world calls great;
Had he lived in pomp and grandeur,
Crown'd with more than royal state;

Still our tongues with praise o'erflowing,
On such boundless love would dwell;
Still our hearts with rapture glowing,
Feel what words could never tell.

But what wonder should it raise,
Thus our lowest state to borrow!
O the high mysterious ways,
God's own Son a child of sorrow!

'Twas to bring us endless pleasure,
He our suffering nature bore;
'Twas to give us heavenly treasure,
He was willing to be poor.

Come, ye rich, survey the stable

Where your infant Saviour lies;
From your full o'erflowing table
Send the hungry good supplies.

Boast not your ennobled stations,
Boast not that you're highly fed;
Jesus, hear it all ye nations,
Had not where to lay his head.

Learn of me, thus cries the Saviour,
If my kingdom you'd inherit;
Sinner, quit your proud behaviour,
Learn my meek and lowly spirit.

Come, ye servants, see your station
Freed from all reproach and shame;
He who purchased your salvation,
Bore a servant's humble name.

Come, ye poor, some comfort gather
Faint not in the race you run,
Hard the lot your gracious Father
Gave his dear, his only Son.

Think, that if your humbler stations,
Less of worldly good bestow,
You escape those strong temptations,
Which from wealth and grandeur flow.

See your Saviour is ascended!
See he looks with pity down!
Trust him, all will soon be mended,
Bear his cross, you'll share his crown.

Sir Eldred Of The Bower: A Legendary Tale: In Two Parts

PART I

There was a young and valiant Knight,
Sir Eldred was his name;
And never did a worthier wight
The rank of knighthood claim.

Where gliding Tay, her stream sends forth,
To feed the neighbouring wood,
The ancient glory of the North,

Sir Eldred's castle stood.

The Knight was rich as Knight might be
In patrimonial wealth;
And rich in nature's gifts was he,
In youth, and strength, and health.

He did not think, as some have thought,
Whom honour never crown'd,
The fame a father dearly bought,
Could make the son renown'd.

He better thought, a noble sire,
Who gallant deeds had done,
To deeds of hardihood should fire
A brave and gallant son.

The fairest ancestry on earth
Without desert is poor;
And every deed of former worth
Is but a claim for more.

Sir Eldred's heart was ever kind,
Alive to Pity's call;
A crowd of virtues grac'd his mind,
He loved, and felt for all.

When merit rais'd the sufferer's name,
He shower'd his bounty then;
And those who could not prove that claim,
He succour'd still as men.

But sacred truth the Muse compels
His errors to impart;
And yet the Muse reluctant tells
The fault of Eldred's heart.

The mild and soft as infant love
His fond affections melt;
Tho' all that kindest spirits prove
Sir Eldred keenly felt:

Yet if the passions storm'd his soul,
By jealousy led on;
The fierce resentment scorn'd control,
And bore his virtues down.

Not Thule's waves so wildly break

To drown the northern shore;
Not Etna's entrails fiercer shake,
Or Scythia's tempests roar.

As when in summer's sweetest day
To fan the fragrant morn,
The sighing breezes softly stray
O'er fields of ripen'd corn;

Sudden the lightning's blast descends,
Deforms the ravag'd fields;
At once the various ruin blends,
And all resistless yields.

But when, to clear his stormy breast,
The sun of reason shone,
And ebbing passions sunk to rest,
And show'd what rage had done:

O then what anguish he betray'd!
His shame how deep, how true!
He view'd the waste his rage had made,
And shudder'd at the view.

The meek-ey'd dawn, in saffron robe,
Proclaim'd the opening day,
Up rose the sun to gild the globe,
And hail the new-born May;

The birds their vernal notes repeat,
And glad the thickening grove,
And feather'd partners fondly greet
With many a song of love:

When pious Eldred early rose
The Lord of all to hail;
Who life with all its gifts bestows,
Whose mercies never fail!

That done -- he left his woodland glade,
And journey'd far away;
He lov'd to court the distant shade,
And thro' the lone vale stray.

Within the bosom of a wood,
By circling hills embrac'd,
A little, modest mansion stood,
Built by the hand of taste:

While many a prouder castle fell,
This safely did endure;
The house where guardian virtues dwell
Is sacred and secure.

Of Eglantine an humble fence
Around the mansion stood,
Which serv'd at once to charm the sense,
And screen an infant wood.

The wood receiv'd an added grace,
As pleas'd it bent to look,
And view'd its ever verdant face
Reflected in a brook:

The smallness of the stream did well
The master's fortunes show;
But little streams may serve to tell
The source from which they flow.

This mansion own'd an aged Knight,
And such a man was he,
As heaven just shows to human sight,
To tell what man should be.

His youth in many a well-fought field
Was train'd betimes to war;
His bosom, like a well-worn shield,
Was grac'd with many a scar.

The vigour of a green old age
His reverend form did bear;
And yet, alas! the warrior-sage
Had drain'd the dregs of care.

And sorrow more than age can break,
And wound its hapless prey,
'Twas sorrow furrow'd his firm cheek,
And turn'd his bright locks grey.

One darling daughter sooth'd his cares,
A young and beauteous dame,
Sole comfort of his failing years,
And Birtha was her name.

Her heart a little sacred shrine,
Where all the Virtues meet,

And holy Hope and Faith divine
Had claim'd it for their seat.

She lov'd to raise her fragrant bower
Of wild and rustic taste,
And there she screen'd each fav'rite flower
From ev'ry ruder blast:

And not a shrub or plant was there
But did some moral yield,
For wisdom, by a father's care,
Was found in ev'ry field.

The trees, whose foliage fell away,
And with the summer died,
He thought an image of decay
Might lecture human pride:

While fair perennial greens that stood,
And brav'd the wintry blast,
As types of the fair mind he view'd,
Which shall for ever last.

He taught her that the gaudiest flowers
Were seldom fragrant found,
But, wasted soon their little powers,
Dropt useless on the ground:

While the sweet-scented rose shall last,
And still retain its power
When life's imperfect day is past,
And beauty's shorter hour.

And here the virgin lov'd to lead
Her inoffensive day,
And here she oft retir'd to read,
And oft retir'd to pray.

Embower'd, she grac'd the woodland shades,
From courts and cities far,
The pride of Caledonian maids,
The peerless northern star.

As shines that bright and lucid star,
The glory of the night,
When beaming thro' the cloudless air,
She sheds her silver light:

So Birtha shone! -- But when she spoke
The Muse herself was heard,
As on the ravish'd air she broke,
And thus her prayer preferr'd:

'O bless thy Birtha, Power Supreme,
In whom I live and move,
And bless me most by blessing him
Whom more than life I love.'

She starts to hear a stranger's voice,
And with a modest grace,
She lifts her meek eye in surprise,
And sees a stranger's face:

The stranger lost in transport stood,
Bereft of voice and power,
While she with equal wonder view'd
Sir Eldred of the bower.

The virgin blush which spreads her cheek
With nature's purest dye,
And all those dazzling beams which break
Like morning from her eye.

He view'd them all, and as he view'd,
Drank deeply of delight;
And still his raptur'd eye pursued,
And feasted on the sight.

With silent wonder long they gaz'd,
And neither silence broke;
At length the smother'd passion blaz'd,
Enamour'd Eldred spoke:

'O sacred Virtue, heav'nly power!
Thy wondrous force I feel:
I gaze, I tremble, I adore,
Yet die my love to tell.

'My scorn has oft the dart repell'd
Which guileful beauty threw;
But goodness heard, and grace beheld,
Must every heart subdue.'

Quick on the ground her eyes were cast,
And now as quickly rais'd:--
Just then her father haply past,

On whom she trembling gaz'd.

Good Ardolph's eye his Birtha meets
With glances of delight;
And thus with courteous speech he greets
The young and graceful Knight:

'O gallant youth, whoe'er thou art,
Right welcome to this place!
There's something rises at my heart
Which says I've seen that face.'

'Thou generous Knight,' the youth rejoin'd,
'Though little known to fame,
I trust I bear a grateful mind--
Sir Eldred is my name.'

'Sir Eldred?' -- Ardolph loud exclaim'd,
'Renown'd for worth and power?
For valour and for virtue famed,
Sir Eldred of the Bower?

'Now make me grateful, righteous Heaven,
As thou art good to me,
Since to my aged eyes 'tis given
Sir Eldred's son to see!'

Then Ardolph caught him by the hand,
And gazed upon his face,
And to his aged bosom strain'd,
With many a kind embrace.

Again he view'd him o'er and o'er,
And doubted still the truth,
And ask'd what he had ask'd before,
Then thus addrest the youth:

'Come now beneath my roof, I pray,
Some needful rest to take,
And with us many a cheerful day
Thy friendly sojourn make.'

He enter'd at the gate straightway
Some needful rest to take;
And with them many a cheerful day
Did friendly sojourn make.

PART II

Once -- in a social summer's walk,
The gaudy day was fled;
They cheated time with cheerful talk
When thus Sir Ardolph said:

'Thy father was the firmest friend
That e'er my beign blest;
And every virtue heaven could send,
Fast bound him to my breast.

'Together did we learn to bear
The casque and ample shield;
Together learn'd in many a war
The deathful spear to wield.

'To make our union still more dear,
We both were doom'd to prove,
What is most sweet and most severe
In heart-dissolving love.

'The daughter of a neighbouring Knight
Did my fond heart engage,
And ne'er did Heaven the virtues write
Upon a fairer page.

'His bosom felt an equal qound,
Nor sigh'd we long in vain;
One summer's sun beheld us bound
In Hymen's holy chain.

'Thou wast Sir Eldred's only child,
Thy father's darling joy;
On me a lovely daughter smiled,
On me a blooming boy.

'But man has woes -- has clouds of care,
That dim his star of life --
My arms received the little pair,
The earth's cold breast my wife.

'Forgive, thou gentle Knight, forgive,
Fond foolish tears will flow;
One day like mine thy heart may heave,
And mourn its lot of wo.

'But grant, kind Heaven! thou ne'er may'st know

The pangs I now impart;
Nor ever feel the parting blow
That rives a husband's heart.

'Beside the blooming banks of Tay;
My angel's ashes sleep;
And wherefore should her Ardolph stay
Except to watch and weep?

'I bore my beauteous babes away
With many a gushing tear;
I left the blooming banks of Tay,
And brought my darlings here.

'I watch'd my little household cares
And form'd their growing youth,
And fondly train'd their infant years
To piety and truth.'

'Thy blooming Birtha here I see,'
Sir Eldred straight rejoin'd;
'But why the son is not with thee,
Resolve my doubting mind.'

When Birtha did the question hear,
She sigh'd, but could not speak:
And many a soft and tender tear
Stray'd down her damask cheek.

Then pass'd o'er good Sir Ardolph's face
A cast of deadly pale;
But soon composed with manly grace,
He thus renew'd his tale:

'For him my heart too much has bled;
For him, my darling son,
Has sorrow prest my hoary head,
But Heaven's high will be done!

'Scarce eighteen winters had revolved,
To crown the circling year,
Before my valiant boy resolved
The warrior's lance to bear.

'For high I prized my native land,
Too dear his fame I held,
T'oppose a parent's stern command,
And keep him from the field.

'He left me -- left his sister too,
Yet tears bedew'd his face --
What could a feeble old man do?
He burst from my embrace.

'O thirst of glory, fatal flame!
O laurels dearly bought!
Yet sweet is death when earn'd with fame--
So virtuous Edwy thought.

'Full manfully the brave boy strove,
Though pressing ranks oppose;
But weak the strongest arm must prove
Against an host of foes.

'A deadly wound my son receives,
A spear assails his side:
Grief does not kill -- for Adolph lives
To tell that Edwy died.

'His long-loved mother died again
In Edwy's parting groan;
I wept for her, yet wept in vain--
I wept for both in one.

'I would have died -- I sought to die,
But Heaven restrain'd the thought,
And to my passion-clouded eye
My helpless Birtha brought.

'When lo! array'd in robes of light,
A nymph celestial came,
She clear'd the mists that dimm'd my sight--
Religion was her name.

'She proved the chastisement divine,
And bade me kiss the rod:
She taught this rebel heart of mine
Submission to its God.

Religion taught me to sustain
What Nature bade me feel;
And Piety relieved the pain
Which Time can never heal.'

He ceased -- with sorrow and delight
The tale Sir Eldred hears;

Then weeping cries -- 'Thou noble Knight,
For thanks accept my tears.

'O Ardolph, might I dare aspire
To claim so bright a boon!--
Good old Sir Eldred was my sire--
And thou hast lost a son.

'And though I want a worthier plea
To urge so dear a cause;
Yet let me to thy bosom be
What once thy Edwy was.

'My trembling tongue its aid denies;
For thou may'st disapprove;
Then read it in my ardent eyes,
Oh! read the tale of love.

'Thy beauteous Birtha!' -- 'Gracious Power
How could I e'er repine,
Cries Ardolph, 'since I see this hour?
Yes -- Birtha shall be thine.'

A little transient gleam of red
Shot faintly o'er her face,
And every trembling feature spread
With sweet disorder'd grace.

The tender father kindly smiled
With fulness of content:
And fondly eyed his darling child,
Who, bashful, blush'd consent.

O then to paint the vast delight
That fill'd Sir Eldred's heart,
To tell the transports of the Knight,
Would mock the Muse's art.

But every kind and gracious soul,
Where gentle passions dwell,
Will better far conceive the whole,
Than any Muse can tell.

The more the Knight his Birtha knew,
The more he prized the maid;
Some worth each day produced to view,
Some grace each hour betray'd.

The virgin too was fond to charm
The dear accomplish'd youth;
His single breast she strove to warm,
And crown'd, with love, his truth.

Unlike the dames of modern days,
Who general homage claim;
Who court the universal gaze,
And pant for public fame.

Then beauty but on merit smiled,
Nor were her chaste smiles sold;
No venal father gave his child
For grandeur, or for gold.

The ardour of young Eldred's flame
But ill could brook delay,
And oft he press'd the maid to name
A speedy nuptial day.

The fond impatience of his breast
'Twas all in vain to hide,
But she his eager suit represt
With modest maiden pride.

When oft Sir Eldred press'd the day
Which was to crown his truth,
The thoughtful Sire would sigh and say,
'O happy state of youth!

'It little recks the woes which wait
To scare its dreams of joy;
Nor thinks to-morrow's alter'd fate
May all those dreams destroy.

'And though the flatterer Hope deceives,
And painted prospects shows;
Yet man, still cheated, still believes,
Till death the bright scene close.

'So look'd my bride, so sweetly mild,
On me her beauty's slave;
But whilst she look'd, and whilst she smiled,
She sunk into the grave.

'Yet, O forgive an old man's care
Forgive a father's zeal:
Who fondly loves, must greatly fear;

Who fears, must greatly feel.

'Once more in soft and sacred bands
Shall Love and Hymen meet;
To-morrow shall unite your hands,
And -- be your bliss complete!'

The rising sun inflamed the sky,
The golden orient blush'd;
But Birtha's cheeks a sweeter die,
A brighter crimson flush'd.

The Priest, in milk-white vestments clad,
Perform'd the mystic rite;
Love lit the hallow'd torch that led
To Hymen's chaste delight.

How feeble language were to speak
Th' immeasurable joy,
That fired Sir Eldred's ardent cheek,
And triumph'd in his eye!

Sir Ardolph's pleasure stood confest,
A pleasure all his own;
The guarded pleasure of a breast
Which many a grief had known.

'Twas such a sober sense of joy
As Angels well might keep;
A joy chastised by piety,
A joy prepared to weep.

To recollect her scatter'd thought,
And shun the noon-tide hour,
The lovely bride in secret sought
The coolness of her Bower.

Long she remain'd -- th' enamour'd Knight,
Impatient at her stay;
And all unfit to taste delight
When Birtha was away;

Betakes him to the secret bower;
His footsteps softly move;
Impell'd by every tender power,
He steals upon his love.

O, horror! horror! blasting sight!

He sees his Birtha's charms,
Reclined with melting fond delight,
Within a stranger's arms.

Wild phrenzy fires his frantic hand;
Distracted at the sight,
He flies to where the lovers stand,
And stabs the stranger Knight.

'Die, traitor, die! thy guilty flames
Demand th' avenging steel!'--
'It is my brother,' she exclaims,
"Tis Edwy -- Oh farewell.'

An aged peasant, Edwy's guide,
The good old Ardolph sought;
He told him that his bosom's pride,
His Edwy he had brought.

O how the father's feelings melt!
How faint, and how revive!
Just so the Hebrew Patriarch felt,
To find his son alive.

'Let me behold my darling's face,
And bless him ere I die!'
Then with a swift and vigorous pace,
He to the bower did hie:

O sad reverse! -- Sunk on the ground;
His slaughter'd son he view'd;
And dying Birtha, close he found,
In brother's blood imbrued.

Cold, speechless, senseless, Eldred near
Gazed on the deed he had done;
Like the blank statue of Despair,
Or Madness graved in stone.

The father saw -- so Jephthah stood,
So turn'd his wo-fraught eye,
When the dear destined child he view'd,
His zeal had doom'd to die.

He look'd the wo he could not speak,
And on the pale corse prest
His wan, discolour'd, dying cheek
And silent, sunk to rest.

Then Bertha faintly rais'd her eye,
Which long had ceased to stream,
On Eldred fix'd, with many a sigh,
Its dim departing beam.

The cold, cold dews of hastening death,
Upon her pale face stand;
And quick and short her failing breath,
And tremulous her hand.

The cold, cold dews of hastening death,
The dim departing eye,
The quivering hand, the short quick breath
He view'd -- and did not die.

He saw her spirit mount in air,
Its kindred skies to seek!
His heart its anguish could not bear,
And yet it would not break.

The mournful Muse forbears to tell
How wretched Eldred died;
She draws the Grecian Painter's veil,
The vast distress to hide.

Yet Heaven's decrees are just and wise,
And man is born to bear:
Joy is the portion of the skies,
Beneath them all is care.

Yet blame not Heaven; 'tis erring man,
Who mars his own best joys;
Whose passions uncontroll'd, the plan
Of promised bliss destroys.

Had Eldred paused, before the blow,
His hand had never err'd;
What guilt, what complicated wo,
His soul had then been spared!

The deadliest wounds with which we bleed,
Our crimes inflict alone;
Man's mercies from God's hand proceed,
His miseries from his own.

The Bleeding Rock: Or, The Metamorphosis Of A Nymph Into Stone

Where beauteous Belmont rears her modest brow
To view Sabrina's silver waves below,
Lived young Ianthe, fair as beauty's Queen;
She reign'd unrivall'd in the sylvan scene;
Here every charm of symmetry and grace,
Which aids the triumph of the fairest face;
With all that softer elegance of mind,
By genius heighten'd, and by taste refined.
Yet early was she doom'd the child of care,
For hapless love subdued th' ill-fated fair.
Ah! what avails each captivating grace,
The form enchanting, or the fairest face!
Or what each beauty of the heaven-born mind,
The soul superior, or the taste refined?

Beauty
but serves destruction to ensure,
And sense, to feel the pang it cannot cure.

Each neighbouring youth aspired to gain her hand,
And many a suitor came from many a land:
But all in vain each neighbouring youth aspired,
And distant suitors all in vain admired.
Averse to hear, yet fearful to offend,
The lover she refused she made a friend:
Her meek rejection wore so mild a face,
More like acceptance seem'd it, than disgrace.

Young Polydore, the pride of rural swains,
Was wont to visit Helmont's blooming plains:
Who has not heard how Polydore could throw
Th' unerring dart to wound the flying doe?
How leave the swiftest at the race behind,
How mount the courser, and outstrip the wind?
With melting sweetness, or with magic fire,
Breathe the soft lute, or sweep the well-strung lyre?
From that famed lyre no vulgar music sprung,
The Graces tun'd it, and Apollo strung.

Apollo too was once a shepherd swain,
And fed the flock, and grac'd the rustic plain,
He taught what charms to rural life belong,
The social sweetness, and the sylvan song;
He taught fair Wisdom in her grove to woo,
Her joys how precious, and her wants how few!
The savage herds in mute attention stood,

And ravish'd Echo fill'd the vocal wood;
The sacred Sisters, stooping from their sphere,
Forgot their golden harps, intent to hear:
Till Heaven the scene survey'd with jealous eyes,
And Jove, in envy, call'd him to the skies.

Young Polydore was rich in large domains,
In smiling pastures, and in flow'ry plains;
With these, he boasted each exterior charm,
To win the prudent, and the cold to warm;
The fairest semblance of desert he bore,
And each fictitious mark of goodness wore;
Could act the tenderness he never felt,
In sorrow soften, and in anguish melt.
The sight elaborate, the fraudful tear,
The joy dissembled, and the well-feign'd fear,
All these were his; and his each treach'rous art
That steals the guileless and unpractis'd heart.

Too soon he heard of fair Ianthe's fame,
'Twas each enamour'd Shepherd's fav'rite theme;
Return'd the rising, and the setting sun,
The Shepherd's fav'rite theme was never done.
They prais'd her wit, her worth, her shape, her air!
And even interior beauties own'd her fair.

Such sweet perfection all his wonder mov'd;
He saw, admired, nay, fancied that he loved:
But Polydore no gen'rous passion knew,
Lost to all truth in feigning to be true.
No lasting tenderness could warm a heart,
Too vain to feel, too selfish to impart.

Cold as the snows of Rhodope descend,
And with the chilling waves of Hebrus blend
So cold the breast where Vanity presides,
And the whole subject soul absorbs and guides.

Too well he knew to make his conquest sure,
Win her soft heart, yet keep his own secure.
So oft he told the well-imagin'd tale,
So oft he swore - how should he not prevail?
The well-imagin'd tale the nymph believ'd;
Too unsuspecting not to be deceiv'd:
She loved the youth, she thought herself beloved,
Nor blush'd to praise whom every maid approved.
The conquest once achiev'd, the brightest fair
When conquer'd, was no longer worth his care:

When to the world her passion he could prove,
Vain of his pow'r, he jested at her love,
The perjured youth, from sad Ianthe far,
To win fresh triumphs, wages cruel war.
With other nymphs behold the wand'rer rove,
And tell the story of Ianthe's love;
He mocks her easy faith, insults her woe,
Nor pities tears himself had taught to flow.
To sad Ianthe soon the tale was borne,
How Polydore to treach'ry added scorn.

And now her eyes'' soft radiance 'gan to fail,
And now the crimson of her cheek grew pale;
The lily there, in faded beauty shows,
Its sickly empire o'er the vanquish'd rose.
Devouring Sorrow marks her for his prey,
And, slow and certain, mines his silent way.
Yet, as apace her ebbing life declined,
Increasing strength sustain'd her firmer mind.
'O had my heart been hard as his,' she cried,
'An hapless victim thus I had not died:
If there be gods, and gods there surely are,
Insulted virtue doubtless is their care.
Then hasten, righteous powers! my tedious fate,
Shorten my woes, and end my mortal date:
Quick let your power transform this failing frame,
Let me be any thing but what I am!
And since the cruel woes I'm doom'd to feel,
Proceed, alas! from having lov'd too well:
Grant me some form where love can have no part,
No human weakness reach my guarded heart;
Where no soft touch of passion can be felt,
No fond affection this weak bosom melt.
If pity has not left your blest abodes,
Change me to flinty adamant, ye gods!
To hardest rock, or monumental stone,
So may I know no more the pangs I've known;
So shall I thus no farther torment prove,
Nor taunting rivals say she died for love:
For sure, if ought can aggravate our woe,
'Tis the feign'd pity of a prosp'rous foe.'
Thus pray'd the nymph - and straight the Pow'rs addrest,
Accord the weeping suppliant's sad request.

Then, strange to tell! if rural folks say true,
To harden'd Rock the stiff'ning damsel grew;
No more her shapeless features can be known,
Stone is her body, and her limbs are stone;

The growing Rock invades her beauteous face,
And quickly petrifies each living grace:
The stone, her stature nor her shape retains,
The Nymph is vanish'd, but the rock remains.
No vestige now of human shape appears,
No cheek for blushes, and no eyes for tears:
Yet - strange the marvels Poets can impart!
Unchang'd, unchill'd, remain'd the glowing heart;
Its vital spirits destin'd still to keep,
It scorn'd to mingle with the marble heap.

When babbling Fame the wondrous tidings bore,
Grief seiz'd the soul of perjur'd Polydore;
And now the falsehood of his soul appears,
And now his broken vows assail his ears.
Appall'd, his smitten fancy seems to view
The nymph so lovely, and the friend so true.
For since her absense, all the virgin train,
His admiration sought to win in vain.

Tho' not to keep him even Ianthe knew,
From vanity alone his falsehood grew:
O let the youthful heart, thus warn'd, beware,
Of vanity, how deep, how wide the snare;
That half the mischiefs youth and beauty know,
From Vanity's exhaustless fountain flow.

Now deep remorse deprives his soul of rest,
And deep compunction wounds his guilty breast;
Then to the fatal spot in haste he flew,
Eager some vestige of the maid to view;
The shapeless Rock he mark'd, but found no trace
Of lost Ianthe's form, Ianthe's face.
He fix'd his streaming eyes upon the stone,
'And take, sweet maid,' he cried, 'my parting groan;
Since we are doom'd thus terribly to part,
No other nymph shall ever share my heart;
Thus only I'm absolv'd' - he rashly cried,
Then plung'd a deadly poniard in his side!
Fainting, the steel he grasp'd, and as he fell,
The weapon pierc'd the Rock he loved so well;
The guiltless steel assail'd the living part,
And stabb'd the vital, vulnerable heart.
And tho' the rocky mass was pale before,
Behold it ting'd with ruddy streams of gore!
The life-blood issuing from the wounded stone,
Blends with the crimson current of his own;
From Polydore's fresh wound it flow'd in part,

But chief emitted from Ianthe's heart.
And tho' revolving ages since have past,
The meeting torrents undiminish'd last:
Still gushes out the sanguine stream amain,
The standing wonder of the stranger swain.

Now once a ear, so rustic records tell,
When o'er the heath resounds the midnight bell;
On eve of midsummer, that foe to sleep,
What time young maids their annual vigils keep,
The tell-tale shrub, fresh gather'd to declare
The swains who false, from those who constant are;
When ghosts in clanking chains the church-yard walk,
And to the wond'ring ear of fancy talk;
When the scar'd maid steals trembling thro' the grove,
To kiss the grave of him who died for love:
When, with long watchings, Care, at length opprest,
Steals broken pauses of uncertain rest;
Nay, Grief short snatches of repose can take,
And nothing but Despair is quite awake:
Then, at the hour, so still, so full of fear,
When all things horrible to thought appear,
Is perjured Polydore observ'd to rove
A ghastly spectre thro' the gloomy grove;
Then to the Rock, the Bleeding Rock repair,
Where, sadly sighing, it dissolves to air,

Still when the hours of solemn rites return,
The village train in sad procession mourn;
Pluck ev'ry weed which might the spot disgrace,
And plant the fairest field-flowers in their place.
Around no noxious plant or flow'ret grows,
But the first daffodil, and earliest rose:
The snow-drop spreads its whitest bosom here,
And golden cowslips grace the vernal year:
Here the pale primrose takes a fairer hue,
And ev'ry violet boasts a brighter blue.
Here builds the wood-lark, here the faithful dove
Laments his lost, or wooes his living love.
Secure from harm is ev'ry hallow'd nest,
The spot is sacred where true lovers rest.
To guard the Rock from each malignant sprite,
A troop of guardian spirits watch by night;
Aloft in air each takes his little stand,
The neighb'ring hill is hence call'd Fairy Land.

Ode To Dragon

Dragon! since lyrics are the mode,
To thee I dedicate my Ode,
And reason good I plead:
Are those who cannot write, to blame
To draw their hopes of future fame,
From those who cannot read?

O could I, like that nameless wight,
Find the choice minute when to write,
The mollia tempora fandi!
Like his my muse should learn to whistle
A true Heroical Epistle,
In strains which never can die.

Father of lyrics, tuneful Horace!
Can thy great shade do nothing for us
To men the British lyre?
Our luckless Bards have broke the strings,
Seiz'd the scar'd muses, pluck'd their wings,
And put out all their fire.

Dragon! thou tyrant of the yard,
Great namesake of that furious guard
That watch'd the fruits Hesperian!
Thy choicer treasures safely keep,
Nor snatch one moment's guilty sleep,

O Dragon! change with me thy fate,
To me give up thy place and state,
And I will give thee mine:
I, left to think, and thou to feed!
My mind enlarged, thy body freed,
How bless'd my lot and thine!

Then shalt thou scent the rich regale
Of turtle and diluting ale,
Nay, share the savoury bit;
And see, what thou hast never seen,
For thou hast but at Hampton been,
A feat devoid of wit.

Oft shalt thou snuff the smoking venison,
Devour'd, alone, by hungry denizen.
So fresh, thou'lt long to tear it;
Though Flaccus tells a different tale
Of social souls who chose it stale,

Because their friends should share it.

And then on me what joys would wait,
Were I the guardian of thy gate,
How useless bolt and latch!
How vain were locks, and bars how vain,
To shield from harm the household train
Whom I, from love, would watch.

Not that 'twould crown with joy my life,
That Bowden, or that Bowden's wife,
Brought me my daily pickings;
Though she, accelerating Fate,
Decrees the scanty mortal date
Of turkeys and of chickens!

Though fired with innocent ambition,
Bowden, great Nature's rhetorician,
More flowers than Burke produces;
And though he's skill'd more roots to find,
Than ever stock'd an Hebrew's mind,
And knows their various uses.

I'd get my master's ways by rote,
Ne'er would I bark at ragged coat,
Nor tear the tatter'd sinner;
Like him, I'd love the dog of merit,
Caress the cur of broken spirit,
And give them all a dinner.

Nor let me pair his blue-eyed Dame
With Venus' or Minerva's name,
One warrior, one coquet;
No; Pallas and the Queen of Beauty
Shunn'd, or betray'd that nuptial duty,
Which she so high has set.

Whene'er I heard the rattling coach
Proclaim their long-desired approach,
How would I haste to greet them!
Nor ever feel I wore a chain,
Till, starting, I perceived with pain
I could not fly to meet them.

The master loves his sylvan shades,
Here, with the nine melodious maids,
His choicest hours are spent:
Yet shall I hear some witling cry,

(Such witling from my presence fly!)
'Garrick will soon repent:

'Again you'll see him, never fear;
Some half a dozen times a year
He still will charm the age;
Accustom'd long to be admired,
Of shades and streams he'll soon be tired,
And languish for the stage.'

Peace! - To his solitude he bears
The full-blown fame of thirty years.
He bears a nation's praise:
He bears his liberal, polish'd mind,
His worth, his wit, his sense refined;
He bears his well-earn'd Bays.

When warm admirers drop a tear
Because this sun has left his sphere,
And set before his time;
I, who have felt and loved his rays,
What they condemn will loudly praise,
And call the deed sublime.

How wise! long pamper'd with applause,
To make a voluntary pause
And lay his laurels down!
Boldly repelling each strong claim,
To dare assert to Wealth and Fame,
'Enough of both I've known.'

How wise! a short retreat to steal,
The vanity of life to feel,
And from its cares to fly;
To act one calm, domestic scene,
Earth's bustle and the grave between,
Retire and learn to die!

The Foolish Traveller; Or, A Good Inn Is A Bad Home

There was a Prince of high degree,
As great and good as Prince could be;
Much power and wealth were in his hand,
With Lands and Lordships at command.

One son, a favourite son, he had,

An idle, thoughtless kind of lad;
Whom, spite of all his follies past,
He meant to make his heir at last.

The son escaped to foreign lands,
And broke his gracious Sire's commands;
Far, as he fancied, from his sight,
In each low joy he took delight.

The youth, detesting peace and quiet,
Indulged in vice, expense, and riot;
Of each wild pleasure rashly tasted,
Till health declined, and substance wasted.

The tender Sire, to pity prone,
Promised to pardon what was done;
And, would he certain terms fulfil,
He should receive a kingdom still.

The youth the pardon little minded,
So much his sottish soul was blinded;
But though he mourn'd no past transgression,
He liked the future rich possession.

He liked the kingdom when obtain'd,
But not the terms on which 'twas gain'd:
He hated pain and self-denial,
Chose the reward, but shunn'd the trial.

He knew his father's power how great,
How glorious too the promised state!
At length resolves no more to roam,
But straight to seek his father's home.

His Sire had sent a friend to say,
He must be cautious on his way;
Told him what road he must pursue,
And always keep his home in view.

The thoughtless youth set out indeed,
But soon he slacken'd in his speed;
For every trifle by the way
Seduced his idle heart astray.

By every casual impulse sway'd,
On every slight pretence he stay'd;
To each, to all, his passions bend,
He quite forgets his journey's end.

For every sport, for every song,
He halted as he pass'd along:
Caught by each idle sight he saw,
He'd loiter e'en to pick a straw.

Whate'er was present seized his soul,
A feast, a show, a brimming bowl;
Contented with this vulgar lot,
His father's house he quite forgot.

Those slight refreshments by the way,
Which were but meant his strength to stay,
So sunk his soul in sloth and sin,
He look'd no farther than his Inn.

His father's friend would oft appear
And sound the promise in his ear;
Oft would he rouse him, 'Sluggard, come!
This is thy Inn, and not thy home.'

Displeased he answers, 'Come what will,
Of present bliss I'll take my fill;
In vain you plead, in vain I hear,
Those joys are distant, these are near.'

Thus perish'd, lost to worth and truth,
In sight of home this hapless youth;
While beggars, foreigners, and poor,
Enjoy'd the father's boundless store.

Application

My Fable, Reader, speaks to thee,
In God this bounteous father see;
And in his thoughtless offspring trace,
The sinful, wayward human race.

The friend, the generous father sent,
To rouse, and to reclaim him, meant;
The faithful minister you'll find,
Who calls the wandering, warns the blind.

Reader, awake! this youth you blame -
Are not you doing just the same?
Mindless your comforts are but given

To help you on your way to heaven.

The pleasures which beguile the road,
The flowers with which your path is strew'd;
To these your whole desires you bend,
And quite forget your journey's end.

The meanest toys your soul entice,
A feast, a song, a game at dice;
Charm'd with your present paltry lot,
Eternity is quite forgot.

Then listen to a warning friend,
Who bids you mind your journey's end;
A wandering pilgrim here you roam;
This world's your Inn, the next your
Home

Inscription On A Cenotaph In A Garden, Erected To A Deceased Friend

Ye lib'ral souls who rev'rence Friendship's name,
Who boast her blessings, and who feel her flame;
Oh! if from early youth one friend you've lov'd,
Whom warm affection chose, and taste approv'd;
If you have known what anguish rends the heart,
When such, so known, so lov'd, for ever part;
Approach! - For you the mourner rears this stone,
To soothe your sorrows, and record his own.

Reflections Of King Hezekiah, In His Sickness

'Set thine house in order, for thou shalt die.' - Isaiah xxxviii.

What! and no more? - Is this, my soul, said I,
My whole of being? - Must I surely die?
Be robbed at once of health, of strength, of time,
Of youth's fair promise, and of pleasure's prime?
Shall I no more behold the face of morn,
The cheerful day-light, and the spring's return?
Must I the festive bower, the banquet leave,
For the dull chambers of the darksome grave?

Have I consider'd what it is to die?
In native dust with kindred worms to lie;

To sleep in cheerless cold neglect! to rot!
My body loath'd, my very name forgot!
Not one of all those parasites, who bend
The supple knee, their monarch to attend!
What, not one friend! No, not a hireling slave
Shall hail great Hezekiah in the grave.
Where's he, who falsely claim'd the name of great?
Whose eye was terror, and whose frown was fate?
Who aw'd a hundred nations from the throne?
See, where he lies, dumb, friendless, and alone!
Which grain of dust proclaims the noble birth?
Which is the royal particle of earth?
Where are the marks, the princely ensigns where?
Which is the slave, and which great David's heir?
Alas! the beggar's ashes are not known
From his who lately sat on Israel's throne!

How stands my great account? My soul, survey
The debt eternal justice bids thee pray!
Should I frail Memory's records strive to blot,
Will Heaven's tremendous reckoning be forgot?
Can I, alas, the awful volume tear?
Or rase one page of the dread register?'
Prepare thy house, thy heart in order set;
Prepare the Judge of Heaven and Earth to meet.
'So spake the warning Prophet. - Awful words:
Which fearfully my troubled soul records.

Am I Prepar'd? And can I meet my doom?
Nor shudder at the dreaded wrath to come?
Is all in order set, my house, my heart?
Does no besetting sin still claim a part?
No cherish'd error, loth to quit its place,
Obstruct within my soul the work of grace?
Did I each day for this great day prepare,
By righteous deeds, by sin-subduing pray'r?
Did I each night, each day's offence repent,
And each unholy thought and word lament?
Still have these ready hands th' afflicted fed,
And minister'd to Want her daily bread?
The cause I knew not did I well explore?
Friend, advocate, and parent of the poor?
Did I, to gratify some sudden gust
Of thoughtless appetite, some impious lust
Of pleasure or of pow'r, such sums employ
As would have flush'd pale penury with joy?
Did I in groves forbidden altars raise,
Or molten gods adore, or idols praise?

Did my firm faith to Heaven still point the way?
Did Charity to man my actions sway?
Did meek-ey'd Patience all my steps attend?
Did generous Candour mark me for her friend?
Did I unjustly seek to build my name
On the pil'd ruins of another's fame?
Did I abhor, as hell, th' insidious lie,
The low deceit, th' unmanly calumny?
Did my fix'd soul the impious wit detest?
Did my firm virtue scorn the unhallow'd jest,
The sneer profane, and the poor ridicule
Of shallow Infidelity's dull school?
Did I still live as born one day to die,
And view th' eternal world with constant eye?

If so I liv'd, if so I kept thy word,
In mercy view, in mercy hear me, Lord!
For oh! how strict soe'er I kept thy law,
From mercy only all my hopes I draw:
My holiest deeds indulgence will require;
The best but to forgiveness will aspire;
If thou my purest services regard,
'Twill be with pardon only, not reward.
How imperfection's stamp'd on all below!
How sin intrudes in all we say or do!
How late in all the insolence of health,
I charm'd th' Assyrian by my boast of wealth
How fondly, with elab'rate pomp, display'd
My glittering treasures! with what triumph laid
My gold and gems before his dazzled eyes,
And found a rich reward in his surprise!
Oh! mean of soul, can wealth elate the heart,
Which of the man himself is not a part!
Oh, poverty of pride! Oh, foul disgrace!
Disgusted Reason, blushing, hides her face.
Mortal, and proud! strange contradicting terms!
Pride for death's victim, for the prey of worms:
Of all the wonders which the eventful life
Of man presents; of all the mental strife
Of warring passions; all the raging fires
Of furious appetites and mad desires;
Not one so strange appears as this alone,
That man is proud of what is not his own.

How short is human life! the very breath
Which frames my words, accelerates my death.
Of this short life how large a portion's fled!
To what is gone I am already dead;

As dead to all my years and minutes past,
As I, to what remains, shall be at last;
Can I past miseries so far forget,
To view my vanish'd years with fond regret?
Can I again my worn-out fancy cheat?
Indulge fresh hope? solicit new deceit?
Of all the vanities weak man admires,
Which greatness gives, youth hopes, or pride desires,
Of these, my soul, which hast thou not enjoy'd?
With each, with all, thy stated pow'rs are cloy'd.
What can I then expect from length of days?
More wealth, more wisdom, pleasure, health, or praise?
More pleasure! hope not that, deluded king;
For when did age increase of pleasure bring?
Is health, of years prolong'd the common breast?
And dear-earn'd Fame, is not cheaply lost?
More Wisdom! that indeed were happiness;
That were a wish a king might well confess;
But when did Wisdom covet length of days?
Or seek its bliss in pleasure, wealth, or praise?
No: - Wisdom views with an indifferent eye
All finite joys, all blessings born to die.
The soul on earth is an immortal guest,
Compell'd to starve at an unreal feast:
A spark, which upward tends by Nature's force;
A stream diverted from its parent source;
A drop dissever'd from the boundless sea;
A moment, parted from eternity;
A pilgrim panting for the rest to come;
An exile, anxious for his native home.

Why should I ask my forfeit life to save?
Is Heav'n unjust which dooms me to the grave?
Was I with hope of endless days deceived?
Or of lov'd life am I alone bereav'd?
Let all the great, the rich, the learn'd, the wise,
Let all the shades of Judah's monarchs rise,
And say, if genius, learning, empire, wealth,
Youth, beauty, virtue, strength, renown, or health,
Has once revers'd the immutable decree
On Adam pass'd, of man's mortality?
What! have these eyes ne'er seen the felon worm
The damask cheek devour, the finish'd form?
On the pale rose of blasted beauty feed,
And riot on the lip so lately red?
Where are our fathers? Where th' illustrious line
Of holy prophets, and of seers divine?
Live they for ever? Do they shun the grave?

Or when did wisdom its professor save?
When did the brave escape? When did the breasts
Of eloquence charm the dull ear of death?
When did the cunning argument avail,
The polish'd period, or the varnish'd tale;
The eye of lightning, or the soul of fire,
Which thronging thousands crowded to admire?
Even while we praise the verse the poet dies;
And silent as his lyre great David lies.
Thou, blest Isaiah! who, at God's command
Now speak'st repentance to a guilty land,
Must die! as wise and good thou had'st not been,
As Nebat's son, who taught the land to sin.

And shall I then be spar'd? Oh monstrous pride!
Shall I escape, when Solomon has died?
If all the worth of all the saints were vain -
Peace, peace, my troubled soul, nor dare complain!
Lord, I submit. Complete thy gracious will;
For if thou slay me, I will trust Thee still.
Oh! be my will so swallow'd up in thine!
That I may do thy will in doing mine.

On The Reverend Sir James Stonhouse, Bart. M.D., In The Chapel At The Hotwells, Bristol

Here rests awhile, in happier climes to shine,
The Orator, Physician, and Divine:
'Twas his, like Luke, the double task to fill,
To heal the nat'ral, and the moral ill.
You, whose awaken'd hearts his labours blest,
Where ev'ry truth by ev'ry grace was drest;
Oh! let your lives evince that still you feel
Th' effective influence of his fervent zeal.
One spirit rescued from eternal woe
Where nobler fame than marble can bestow;
That lasting monument will mock decay,
And stand, triumphant, at the final day.

On The Reverend Mr. Love, In The Cathedral At Bristol

When worthless grandeur fills th' embellish'd urn,
No poignant grief attends the sable bier;
But when distinguish'd excellence we mourn,
Deep is the sorrow, genuine is the tear.

Stranger! should'st thou approach this awful shrine,
The merits of the honour'd dead to seek;
The friend, the son, the Christian, the divine,
Let those who knew him, those who lov'd him, speak.

O let him in some pause of anguish say,
What zeal inflam'd, what faith enlarg'd his breast;
How glad th' unfetter'd spirit wing'd its way
From earth to heav'n, from blessing to be blest!

On The Reverend Mr. Hunter, Who Received A Degree From The University Of Oxford

Go, happy spirit, seek that blissful land
Where zealous Michael leads the glorious band
Of those who fought for truth; blest spirit, go,
And perfect all the good begun below;
Go hear applauding Saints, delighted, tell
How vanquish'd Falsehood, at thy bidding, fell!
Blest in that heav'n whose paths thy virtue sought;
Blest in that God whose cause thou well hast fought;
O let thy honour'd shade his care approve,
Who this memorial rears of filial love:
A son, whose father, living, was his pride;
A son, who mourns that such a father died.

On Sarah Stonhouse, Second Wife Of The Rev. Sir James Stonhouse, Bart

Come, Resignation! wipe the human tear,
Domestic anguish drops o'er Virtue's bier;
Bid selfish sorrow hush the fond complaint,
Nor, from the God she lov'd, detain the saint.
Truth, meekness, patience, honour'd shade! were thine;
And holy hope, and charity divine:
Tho' these thy forfeit being could not save
Thy faith subdued the terrors of the grave.

Oh! if thy living excellence could teach,
Death has a loftier emphasis of speech:
Let death thy strongest lesson then impart,
And write, prepare to die on every heart.

On Mrs Little, In Redcliff Church, Bristol

O could this verse her fair example spread,
And teach the living while it prais'd the dead!
Then, reader, should it speak her hope divine,
Not to record her faith, but strengthen thine;
Then should her ev'ry virtue stand confest,
Till ev'ry virtue kindled in thy breast.
But if thou slight the monitory strain,
And she has liv'd, to thee at least, in vain;
Yet let her death, an awful lesson give,
The dying Christian speaks to all that live.
Enough for her that here her ashes rest,
Till God's own plaudit shall her worth attest.

On Mrs Blandford

Meek shade, farewell! go seek that quiet shore
Where sin shall vex, and sorrow wound no more;
Thy lowly worth obtains that final bliss,
Which pride disdains to seek, and wit may miss.
That path thou'st found, which science cannot teach,
But faith and goodness never fail to reach;
Then share the joy the words of life impart,
The Vision promis'd to the
pure in heart

On General Lawrence

Born to command to conquer, and to spare,
As mercy mild, yet terrible as war,
Here Lawrence rests in death; while living fame
From Thames to Ganges wafts his honour'd name.
To him this frail memorial Friendship rears,
Whose noblest monument's a nation's tears:
Whose deeds on fairer columns stand engrav'd,
In Province preserv'd, and Cities saved.

Epitaph: On the Reverend Mr Penrose

If social manners, if the gentlest mind,
If zeal for God, and love for human kind,
If all the charities which life endear,

May claim affection, or demand a tear,
Then, o'er Penrose's venerable urn
Domestic love may weep, and friendship mourn.

The path of duty still, untired, he trod,
He walk'd in safety, for he walk'd with God!
When past the power of precept and of prayer
Yet still his flock remain'd the shepherd's care;
Their wants still kindly watchful to supply,
He taught his best, last lesson, how to die?

Faith and Works – A Tale

Good Dan and Jane were man and wife,
And lived a loving kind of life.
One point, however, they disputed
And each by turns his mate confuted.
'Twas Faith and Works, this knotty question,
They found not easy of digestion.
While Dan for Faith alone contended,
Jane equally Good Works defended.
'They are not Christians, sure, but Turks,
Who build on Faith and scoff at Works,'
Quoth Jane; while eager Dan replied,
'By none but Heathens Faith's denied.
I'll tell you, wife,' one day quoth Dan,
'A story of a right good man:
A Patriarch sage, of ancient days,
A man of Faith whom all must praise;
In his own country he possess'd
Whate'er can make a wise man blest,
His was the flock, the field, the spring,
In short, a little rural king.
Yet pleas'd he quits his native land,
By Faith in the Divine command.
God bade him go; and he, content,
Went forth, not knowing where he went:
He trusted in the promise made,
And, undisputing, straight obey'd.
The heavenly word he did not doubt,
But proved his Faith by going out.'
Jane answer'd with some little pride:
'I've an example on my side;
And though my tale be somewhat longer,
I trust you'll find it vastly stronger.
I'll tell you, Daniel, of a man,

The holiest since the world began
Who now God's favour is receiving,
For prompt obeying, not believing.
One only son this man possess'd,
In whom his righteous age was blest;
And more to mark the grace of heaven
This son by miracle was given.
And from this child, the word Divine,
Had promised an illustrious line.
When lo! at once a voice he hears,
Which sounds like thunder in his ears!
God says, 'Go sacrifice thy son!'
'This moment, Lord, it shall be done.'
He goes, and instantly prepares,
To slay this child of many pray'rs,
Now here you see the grand expedience,
Of Works, of actual, sound obedience.
This was not Faith, but act and deed;
The Lord commands the child shall bleed:
Thus Abraham acted,' Jenny cried,
'Thus Abraham trusted,' Dan replied.
'Abraham!' quoth Jane, 'why that's my man.'
'No, Abraham's he I mean,' says Dan.
'He stands a monument of Faith.'
'No, 'tis for Works the Scripture saith.'
''Tis for Obedience I commend him.'
Thus he, thus she; both warmly feel,
And lose their temper in their zeal.
Too quick each other's choice to blame,
They did not see each meant the same.
At length, 'Good wife,' said honest Dan,
'We're talking of the self-same man.
The Works you praise, I own indeed,
Grow from that Faith for which I plead.
And Abraham, whom for Faith I quote
For Works deserves especial note.
'Tis not enough of Faith to talk:
A man of God with God must walk.
Our doctrines are at last the same,
They only differ in the name.
The Faith, I fight for, is the root;
The Works, you value, are the fruit.
How shall you know my creed's sincere,
Unless in Works my Faith appear?
How shall I know a tree's alive,
Unless I see it bear and thrive?
Your Works not growing on my root,
Would prove they were not genuine Fruit.

If Faith produce no Works, I see,
That Faith is not a living tree.
Thus Faith and Works together grow;
No separate life they e'er can know.
They're soul and body, hand and heart;
What God hath join'd let no man part!'

Hannah More - A Short Biography

Hannah More was born on February 2nd, 1745 at Fishponds in the parish of Stapleton, near Bristol. She was the fourth of five daughters of Jacob More, a schoolmaster. He was originally from a family of Presbyterians in Norfolk, but had become a member of the Church of England to pursue a career in the Church. After losing a lawsuit over an estate he had hoped to inherit, he moved to Bristol, becoming an excise officer and later a teacher at the Fishponds free school.

The City of Bristol, at that time, was a centre for slave-trading and Hannah would, over time, become one of its staunchest critics.

The More's were a close family and all the sisters were educated at first by their father who taught them Latin and mathematics. Hannah was also taught French by her elder sisters. Her conversational French was improved by time spent with French prisoners of war from the Seven-Year's-War in Frenchay, then a small village near Bristol.

She was keen to learn, possessed a sharp intellect and was assiduous in studying and, according to family tradition, began writing at an early age.

In 1758 Jacob established his own girls' boarding school at Trinity Street in Bristol for the elder sisters, Mary and Elizabeth, to run. Hannah became a pupil there when she was 12. Jacob and his wife moved to Stony Hill in the city to open a school for boys.

Hannah became a teacher at her sister's school and it was here that she produced her first literary efforts. These were prompted by trying to find material suitable for her young charges to act in. Her first, written in 1762, was The Search after Happiness (by the mid-1780s some 10,000 copies had been sold).

In 1767 Hannah gave up her share in the school to become engaged to William Turner. After six years, with no wedding in sight, and Turner reluctant to move forward, the engagement was broken off. It was now 1773 and by all accounts Hannah suffered a nervous breakdown and spent some time recuperating in nearby Uphill. Turner then bestowed upon her an annual annuity of £200. This was enough to meet her needs and set her free to pursue a literary career. With that ambition London was her next stop. She travelled there in the winter of 1773/74 together with her sisters, Sarah and Martha.

She had previously written some verses on a production of King Lear staged by the famous actor David Garrick and this led to a lasting friendship with him and a pivotal introduction to the London Literary society. Now she met and charmed Samuel Johnson, Joshua Reynolds and Edmund Burke. Johnson is quoted as saying to her "Madam, before you flatter a man so grossly to his face, you should consider whether or not your flattery is worth having." He would later be quoted as calling her "the finest versifatrix in the English language".

Hannah also became a leading member of the Bluestocking group of women who met to further literary and intellectual pursuits. Here she met women who were to become life-long friends; Elizabeth Montagu, Frances Boscawen, Elizabeth Carter, Elizabeth Vesey and Hester Chapone (Hannah later wrote a celebration of this circle in her 1782 poem The Bas Bleu, or, Conversation, published in 1784).

Her first play, The Inflexible Captive, was staged at Bath in 1775. It was based on the opera, Attilio Regulo, by the Italian Pietro Metastasio (1698-1782) whose works she admired.

Her theatrical career was now in full swing. David Garrick himself produced her next play, Percy, in 1777 as well as writing both the Prologue and Epilogue for it. It was a great success when performed at Covent Garden in December of that year. Her next play, Fatal Falsehood, was staged in 1779, shortly after the death of Garrick. It was less successful but still admired.

With David Garrick now passed (January 20th, 1779) Hannah came to view the theatre as both morally wrong and not where her ambitions now lay. She now began to spend her time advancing her interests in other areas.

In 1781 she first met Horace Walpole, man of letters art historian and Whig politician and now corresponded regularly with him.

A friendship with James Oglethorpe, who had long been concerned with slavery as a moral issue and who was working with Granville Sharp in an early abolitionist capacity, started to awaken Hannah's social conscious.

Hannah turned to religious writing, beginning with her Sacred Dramas in 1782; it rapidly ran through nineteen editions. These and the poems Bas-Bleu and Florio (1786) mark her gradual transition to a more serious and considered view of life and are fully expressed in her Thoughts on the Importance of the Manners of the Great to General Society (1788), and An Estimate of the Religion of the Fashionable World (1790).

In Bristol, in 1784, she discovered the poet Ann Yearsley, the so-called 'poetical milkmaid of Bristol'. With Yearsley destitute, Hannah raised a considerable sum of money for her. Lactilia, as Yearsley was known, published Poems, on Several Occasions in 1785, earning about £600. Hannah and Elizabeth Montagu held the profits in trust to protect them from Yearsley's husband. However Ann wished for the capital to be made over, and made insinuations of stealing against Hannah. The money was released and Hannah felt her reputation had been tarnished.

With the death of Samuel Johnson in December 1784, Hannah moved, with her sister Martha, in 1795, to a cottage at Cowslip Green, near Wrington in rural Somerset, "to escape from the world gradually".

In the summer of 1786, she spent time with Sir Charles and Lady Margaret Middleton at their home in Teston in Kent. Among their guests was the local vicar James Ramsay and a young Thomas Clarkson, both of whom were central to the early abolition campaign against slavery.

In 1787, she met John Newton and the 'Clapham Sect' (a group of wealthy evangelical Christians who lived near Clapham and met at Henry Thornton's house). The group was strongly opposed to the Slave Trade. William Wilberforce was a member of the group and he and Hannah became firm friends.

Hannah contributed much to the running of the newly-founded Abolition Society including, in February 1788, her publication of Slavery, a Poem which has long been recognised as one of the most important poems of the abolition period. The poem dramatically described a mistreated, enslaved female separated from her children and severely questioned Britain's role in the Slave Trade.

Her relationship with members of the society, especially Wilberforce, was close. She spent the summer of 1789 holidaying with Wilberforce in the Peak District, planning for the abolition campaign, which, at the time, was at its height.

Her work now became more evangelical. In the 1790s she wrote several Cheap Repository Tracts which covered moral, religious and political topics and were both for sale or distributed to literate poor people. This coincided with her increasing philanthropic work in the Mendip area.

Beyond any doubt, Hannah was the most influential female member of the Society for Effecting the Abolition of the African Slave Trade.

Hannah wrote many ethical books and tracts: Strictures on the Modern System of Female Education (1799), Hints towards Forming the Character of a Young Princess (1805), Cœlebs in Search of a Wife (only nominally a story, 1809), Practical Piety (1811), Christian Morals (1813), Character of St Paul (1815), Moral Sketches (1819). She was a rapid writer, and her work is consequently discursive, animated and without a rigorous structure.

However the originality and force of Hannah's writings perhaps explains her extraordinary popularity. At the behest of Beilby Porteus, Bishop of London and a leading abolitionist, Hannah wrote many spirited rhymes and prose tales, the earliest of which was Village Politics, by Will Chip (1792), intended to counteract the doctrines of Thomas Paine and the influence of the French Revolution.

The series of Cheap Repository Tracts, eventually led to the formation of the Religious Tracts Society. The Tracts were produced at the rate of three a month between 1795 and 1797.

The most famous is perhaps The Shepherd of Salisbury Plain, describing a family of incredible frugality and contentment. Two million copies of these rapid and telling sketches were circulated, in one year, teaching the poor in rhetoric of the most ingenious homeliness to rely upon the virtues of content, sobriety, humility, industry and reverence for the British Constitution, hatred of the French, trust in God and in the kindness of the gentry.

Several of the Tracts oppose slavery and the slave trade, in particular, the poem The Sorrows of Yamba; or, The Negro Woman's Lamentation, which appeared in November 1795 and which was co-authored with Eaglesfield Smith. However, the tracts have also been noted for their encouragement of social quietism in an age of revolution.

In 1789, she purchased a small house at Cowslip Green in Somerset. Wilberforce encouraged Hannah to set up a Sunday school in Cheddar, where poor children could be taught to read. Soon she and her sisters had set up similar schools throughout the Mendip villages, despite fierce opposition.

She was instrumental in setting up twelve schools by 1800 where reading, the Bible and the catechism were taught to local children. Hannah also donated money to Bishop Philander Chase for the founding of Kenyon College, and a portrait of her hangs there in Peirce Hall.

John Scandrett Harford of Blaise Castle was a prodigious benefactor to More's schools in the 1790s, and Hannah modeled the idealised hero and heroine in Cœlebs in Search of Wife (1809) on Mr and Mrs Harford.

However it cannot be said that Hannah was a staunch supporter of Women's rights. She refused to read Mary Wollstonecraft's Rights of Women, saying "so many women are fond of government... because they are not fit for it. To be unstable and capricious is but too characteristic of our sex". She was also shocked by the movement for female education in France, saying "they run to study philosophy, and neglect their families to be present at lectures in anatomy". She is also said to have turned down an honorary membership of the Royal Society of Literature because she considered her "sex alone a disqualification".

The More sisters also met with a good deal of opposition in their philanthropic works: the farmers thought that education, even to the limited extent of learning to read, would be fatal to agriculture, and the clergy, whose neglect she was making good, accused her of Methodist tendencies.

She continued to oppose slavery throughout her life, but at the time of the Abolition Bill of 1807 (which outlawed the slave trade, but not slavery itself), her health did not permit her to take as active a role in the movement as she had done in the late 1780s, although she maintained a correspondence with Wilberforce and others Abolitionists.

In her later life, she continued to dedicate much of her time to religious writing. Nevertheless, her most popular work was a novel, Cœlebs in Search of a Wife, which appeared in two volumes in 1809 (and which ran to nine editions in 1809 alone).

In 1816, Hannah was still at odds with the French. Following Waterloo she is quoted as saying that 'peace with France is a worse evil than war', and refused to allow a French translation of Cœlebs.

Her last few years were spent at Clifton, people from all parts came to visit her even though her health was fading and she was writing less often.

She lived just long enough to see the act finally abolishing slavery. In July 1833, the Bill to abolish slavery throughout the British Empire passed in the House of Commons, followed by the House of Lords on August 1st.

Hannah More died on September 7th, 1833. She is buried at Church of All Saints, Wrington. In her will she left more than £30,000 to charities and religious societies, the equivalent today of many millions.

www.ingramcontent.com/pod-product-compliance
Lightning Source LLC
Chambersburg PA
CBHW060139050426
42448CB00010B/2199